Infinite Manifesting

From Infinite Possibilities

AnnaMarie Antoski

Copyright © 2011 AnnaMarie Antoski

All rights reserved.

ISBN-13: 978-1460914403

DEDICATION

This is dedicated to You!

The Infinite Being of you that is consciously choosing to evolve through your physical embodiment.

Knowing that you are deserving of everything you could ever desire because it's your divine birth heritage.

Disclaimer :
The information in this book and the author holds no responsibility for your own choices for medical attention, assistance or medication.

CONTENTS

	Acknowledgments	i
1	Infinite Manifesting	1
2	My Psychic Evolution	6
3	I-M Introduction	11
4	Infinite Thoughts	16
5	Infinite Creators	21
6	Observer Effect	31
7	Appreciation, Count your Blessings	37
8	Your First Awakening Thoughts	41
9	Finite and Infinite Creations	45
10	Ego or Infinite Being	50
11	Powerful Purposes in Challenges	54
12	Infinite Possibilities	61
13	Infinite Abilities	65
14	Quantum Living	73
15	Practicing the Paranormal	79
16	Self Healing	86
17	Hooponopono	95
18	Psychic Children	101
19	Synchronicity	103
20	Creating Your Own Affirmations	108

21	Infinite Words Matter	112
22	Hidden Meanings in Words	118

Part Two Psychic Experiences

1	Out of Body	127
2	Telepathy	133
3	Fire Walk	139
4	Spirit Communication	143
5	Breaking Arrow with Throat	149
6	Spoon Bending	152
7	Mastering Cards	156
8	Telekinesis	160
9	Shifting Realities	165

Part Three Helpful Knowledge

1	Our Brain Rewires Itself	177
2	Create Your Day Your Way	181
3	Emotional Addiction	184
4	Subconscious Mind	188
5	Everything is Neutral	194
6	Level of Acceptance	198
7	Letting Go	202
8	Beliefs about Wealth	213
9	Lottery as Feedback	221
10	Evolving to Sovereignty	229

ACKNOWLEDGMENTS

With great love and appreciation I would like to thank my family and friends who have allowed me to be who I am with no conditions and just pure loving acceptance.

I would also like to thank with great appreciation all the inspirational authors, teachers and masters who have lead the way with their exuberance and wisdom.

PART ONE

THE EVOLVING JOURNEY OF INFINITE MANIFESTING

The journey begins as we remember

who we really are as infinite beings

experiencing physical reality

Chapter 1

✳ ✳ ✳ ✳ ✳ ✳ ✳ ✳ ✳ ✳ ✳ ✳

INFINITE MANIFESTING

Since you are reading this then we must be on a similar vibration for you to have attracted this book to you. I know you will enjoy the journey into all possibilities where nothing is impossible unless we believe it to be and if that is the case then all beliefs can be restructured to support all new possibilities. I am so glad and appreciative that you are coming along this infinite manifesting journey. As you read along as I share with you my own evolving journey of experiences into the unknown that I have become to know and if there are still some experiences that you have not experienced it gives you a head up, so to speak of similar occurrences.

This book is a result from many requests I received to have my website transformed into book form and of course you will find more information, video's and links on the website .

As you share in this journey, it will lead you into the exploration into experiencing and knowing more of our amazing capabilities that are available to use. I am quite sure that even as I write this more infinite capabilities will be known as more individuals evolve on the leading edge of making more unknown known for us all. When we approach it all with an open mind into infinite consciousness where everything is possible then it's quite the eternal evolving journey to be on.

I'd like to also mention that whenever I use the label's of psychic, paranormal, extraordinary, ESP and any psychic ability it can all really just be merged into containing one label Infinite Abilities or ESP. Infinite Abilities describes choosing thoughts from the higher dimensional vibrations of consciousness compared to the lower dimensional frequency's. And ESP is another favorite because the word describes extra sensory perception, so throughout this book I do use many of the different definitions, but these are just different labels describing the same thing. Higher infinite consciousness allows us to choose from all possibilities to experiencing amazing abilities in our physical experiences.

Regardless when you are reading this, in the infinite realm there is no separation of time and space. So I am writing this in my present and you will be reading it in my future in your present or maybe even many years or decades from now, it doesn't matter. It's the energy that is still contained within this book and also a connection to all who read it too. For everyone who reads this book will also change the energy of it in invisible yet infinite amazing ways that we are not even aware of, since everything is energy.

This is evolving and ancient wisdom that I am sure will sustain the ages just as all greatest wisdom does. There will always be others interested in going beyond normal conditioning limited beliefs and into the unlimited journey of making the unknown known.

This book is an accumulation of great teachings from many great teachers that I have implemented their teachings in my own life as you will read on my about chapter and throughout this book. It's all proof for me that all that has and is taught that I share with you is true, it works when we work it. Though different teachers teach many of the same teachings or ancient wisdom adding their own wisdom and blended flavor they are all really teaching similar teachings. It allows such a variety that for anyone interested there are now so much more to choose from in the learning processes and that is so fantastic. So when we need repetition we have a great variety now to choose from along our journey. But the best part will always be your own experiences from any teaching because it will be evidence for yourself that the wisdom does work.

When we come to realize that OUR THOUGHTS DO MATTER, that our thoughts are energy is when we have begun the process of opening to more wonderful sovereignty for ourselves.

Just think for a moment of how a small squirt of dish soap added into water and observe all the bubbles that form from it, thousands of them expanding just from one little squirt. It reminds me of how our thoughts expand the same way depending on our most dominant thoughts throughout our day. It is the thoughts we are choosing that creates what becomes what we feel that's our "observer effect" in how our days unfold into our creations being manifested.

Everything is Possible

As we continue to consciously choose thoughts from the infinite consciousness then everything and anything is Possible. It is possible because in the infinite dimensions of no time it exists or we would not be able to think it, which is the reason it IS possible. So that leaves nothing out. When your belief transforms to knowing then nothing will stop you from experiencing what you want.

Why is learning and using your psychic or supernormal abilities important?

Infinite manifesting is when we go beyond to experience abilities that we have not experienced in our past. To know more about our own self and the amazing abilities we can experience and use, about our body and its well being and experiencing more bliss and knowledge in our daily lives. Infinite manifesting from infinite consciousness is using your psychic abilities as part of evolving into becoming more. We will experience powers that have been latent awaiting activation to use.

We are connecting and being influenced from our infinite being or infinite source instead of our surviving ego personality. Eventually the ego will merge while we evolve into powerful, united, harmonious beings. Our life of challenges will transforms to empowering ways of living in ease. Our life becomes literally magical. When we know we are the creators of our reality and that our thoughts do matter and are triggering the emotions we then feel, we become empowered and vibrate on a higher frequency. We finally remember what we came here to do and who we really are while evolving into our higher powerful being self through our physical body.

A Relative from Our Past

Let us envision for a moment that a relative from our past three hundred years ago was able to visit with us and see things from their perspective. How would they perceive what is going on with their limited thoughts of beliefs when they see us staring at a big screen hanging on our wall? Then using a device, our cordless converter we have in our hand that changes the motion of pictures on the screen numerous times. They would see us so involved in what is playing on the screen, if we are watching a comedy show they would see us laughing. Especially when no one else is in the room as we interact with that hanging slim box on the wall. The phone rings and you pick up your cell phone and start talking and then walk over to your microwave that you had put popcorn in for three minutes and take it out.

Think about what they would be thinking? They would think you were a wizard or a witch using magic and instantaneously interacting with everything. Your past relative would be so perplexed and the shock of them trying to comprehend it all would be overwhelming.

Your relative would be even more amazed if you were to take them in one of your vehicles and drive them to an airport or watch a jet flying above in the air. Just think about how they would evaluate and judge what was going on. We can use the above analogy the same way we would when we perceive or experience any psychic phenomenon or super infinite abilities that is from infinite manifesting source. When we experience any of these on a regular basis for our self then any perception of paranormal becomes normal for us. Just as in our example with our distant relative, except if you find it impossible then you become the distant relative perceiving the paranormal in a similar way. Our life and our own self becomes unlimited and incredible, feelings of bliss can become everyday experiences because our thoughts create those feelings for us to experience naturally as we evolve.

We become to live the life we dreamed to live and experience heavenly bliss on earth.

So if you're ready, let's begin the journey and have fun doing it. Whatever the challenge we can turn it all into exciting opportunities to sustain ourselves through practicing until we experience any infinite abilities.

CHAPTER 2

* * * * * * * * * * * *

MY PSYCHIC EVOLUTION

I have studied the nature of reality from the best teachers for over twenty years which lead me to knowledge that evolved into the psychic and paranormal. We all have these powers within us, it is not until we start to use them and through experiencing those powers that we then know it for our own self. Our own experiences will always be our own feedback and proof for our self regardless of what anyone else from the normal conscious beliefs may deny. When we experience it for our own self there is never any denial, we can not deny something we experience instead those experiences evolve to more unlimited potential abilities.

When I experience any psychic experience it has shown me how anything that my limited self once believed was labeled impossible or crazy becomes normal, so it is the paranormal becoming normally accepted for us. The more we practice to experience the paranormal for our self the more wisdom we gain and the more we desire to expand to experience more of the psychic abilities. We all experiences glimpses or glitches of psychic abilities throughout our lives but it's when we limit the experience by labeling or define it as not important or valid that can stop us from going further with it. If we let our self expand these abilities to experience more of it until we begin to realize how normal these abilities will become for us. Then we make a quantum leap into the leading edge of consciousness from the limited vibrations to desire to experience more.

That is what I have experienced from the first time that I was able to twist spoons around three and four times, to feel the metal become like soft warm putty showed me through my experience how mutable reality really is. Then when I spent the valuable time needed for me to experience telekinesis bending metal without any physical touch or force, to be able to bend it with my energy focused intention. To watch it bend over an inch and then another inch is just so empowering. I am still working on being able to do it within a few minutes instead of what now takes me over an hour to do. And I am still working on many extraordinary practices to eventually master successfully. There are now many psychic children and adults who naturally use many of these abilities that are so extraordinary and powerfully amazing and they can be our role models for our evolving future.

Now I am able to observe my reality and see my creations manifesting faster then ever before, the linear time gap is lessening with each evolving step I take. Many paranormal abilities that were unknown to me in the past are becoming normal on a daily basis. We all have the potential to become the evolved being in our life's journey.

Shifting Into Changes

From my divorce I became a single mom. Every challenge and struggle became a catalyst for another opportunity to shift my thinking from limited thoughts to unlimited thoughts. Through it all I became to know what I wanted and by being aware of my thoughts on a daily basis was the way to creating my life to be the way I wanted it to be.

I am now in a relationship that continues to evolve and expand with the freedom to be myself that I did not have in previous relationships. I also worked at a job for nineteen years and even though I enjoyed it and put 100% into it and met the most amazing people that became friends, but it was not my true passion. Now I can do what I love to do which is my passion and that passion sustains and expands my inspiration to write when the flow comes through. And experience extraordinary abilities by practicing. It was the help of Site Build It to take something that I love to do and transform it into a website and book with no website building knowledge. Now I start my day doing what I love to do.

It was not always this way, in the past I became depressed very easily because I was not aware of all that I do know now. And of course that created many illnesses that was an ongoing for many of those years. It then became all about self healing for me in the beginning of my learning because that was what I needed and wanted the most, it was my first priority. It was from there that all the other evolving knowledge became to just manifest into my reality to learn from. To experience and know that we are all creator's creating our reality by what we choose to believe from our thoughts. As we change our thoughts then our beliefs change too and that changes our lives.

It was a truly exuberant fulfilling journey during the years and now it's even more fulfilling and exciting as I am still learning the knowledge about the nature of reality. The wisdom I gained from all the experiences along the way changed everything for me to really live each day blissfully.

Blissful Days from Blissful Thinking

Now I am blissful every day. It does not matter what is going on around me, which of course continuously changes to more blissful vibrations. From observing everything as an opportunity for me to evolve into more and constantly use everything as an opportunity to transform everything into my preference.

My desire of owning a home in the country, something I had desired for years is now my reality. But it took me to learn to become one through focus with the home I wanted and for it be become manifested. It has hundreds of acres of land all around us and surrounded by trees and small forests. With a variety of animals that live in the forests and graze sometimes close to the house, I feel one with nature. My life continually unfolds from what I desire into manifested reality. It is from choosing what I refer to as infinite thoughts that keep me focused on the possibilities of everything.

To now live each day in the present with genuine gratitude and appreciation, my heart and health is in harmony with my bliss. From a very unhealthy state of being in my past to now being healthy because I choose thoughts from the infinite source that triggers blissful feelings. I deal with any disharmony in my body in the sovereign ways. I have not been to a doctor or taken any medication for over twenty years and have learned to trust myself and my own diagnosis. If I create any thing out of alignment in my body that creates ill health or pain, I can easily and naturally bring it back into harmony and health.

Now it is natural for me to think, feel and experience my days in bliss and I actually do count my blessings all the time, I have found as a result I can so easily tune into my higher self or infinite source and when I do my creativity flows. This is all a result of choosing from the infinite consciousness of all possibilities where everything is possible for our choosing.

Chapter 3

I-M
INTRODUCTION

I choose I-M ... the short form for Infinite Manifesting as my label and concept because it represents the Infinite as the higher consciousness of thoughts, vibrations, dimensions where everything is unified, connected, everything is possible. More of the invisible becomes visible and manifesting from the infinite expands us to experience what was once unknown to become known through our experiences.

Infinite Manifesting is seeing through the illusions to knowing that we do create all of our reality, we always have and always will. To use the analogy of comparing it to the highest mountain compared to the lowest valley is to see more of reality then we could ever even imagine compared to social conditioning consciousness versus infinite consciousness.

Finite represents manifesting from the social conditioned consciousness that is very limited, doubtful of making the impossible possible, it's filled with fears and doubts and much skepticism. It's so amazing that we have always created our personal reality and adding to mass reality throughout our physical life. Until we become to know this wisdom it's still unconscious because we are unaware and we are limiting ourselves to remain in finite consciousness.

So we are either creating what we prefer to experience and if it's not what we prefer then we use the contrast to show us what we don't want. While still being appreciative for the contrast so that we can then go on to create what we do want and prefer. Infinite Manifesting, I-M is to consciously expand into knowing more then we already know and continuing to do so. It is also transforming all low vibrations of reactions into higher vibrations of energy frequencies to responding and sustaining it until it becomes a natural habit. The difference is amazing and does affect our body, our perceptions, our experiences which completely changes our reality literally. Allowing our self to vibrate on the higher vibrations is the most magnificent experience in every way.

I-M became My Reminder throughout the Day, especially in the Beginning Stages

I created I-M, Infinite Manifesting as a trigger to remind me throughout the day when I found myself reverting back to the old way, old programs of automatic reacting. I would literally SNAP my fingers back and forth with my hands. Then I would change my thoughts back into the infinite way of thinking and then my emotions would become also of a great feeling. It amazed me how quickly it anchored the associate with the Infinite and then I would even carry a rhythmic tune of snapping. To this day my African Gray bird still dances when I do it and gets all happy too.

So I-M is my reminder to know I always do have the choice to choose what thoughts that will create the feelings I do prefer of the higher vibrations from higher consciousness. Eventually it will lead to evolving to using more of our brains abilities and more of our whole self's abilities which are labeled or referred to as psychic, paranormal, ESP or extraordinary abilities.

As usual in the limited consciousness everything is labeled and separated, however in the higher infinite consciousness everything becomes more unified and whole. So instead of separating all our extraordinary abilities into separate labels as ESP, telekinesis, premonition, out of body, lucid dreaming, future predictions, remote viewing, mind through matter and so on, it will all be merged into One Extraordinary Sense of Evolved Perception. So ESP could explain to define all extraordinary abilities.

Mirror Reflection Work is Letting go of our Past and Creating Infinite Memories

I found the difference was so amazing coming from victim beliefs and transforming the knowledge into wisdom. Though it did take quite a journey through all the years of experiences, but it did prove to me that we really do create all of our reality and the infinite is the way to go. Any parts of our reality we deny that we created it is just another part of our subconscious programming we have not cleaned up or transformed yet.

All reflections that another person or a situations or experiences that would trigger a negative or low vibration reaction was what I would work on.

I referred to it as reflection work and used Wayne Dyer's analogy of the orange, "when we squeeze an orange, orange juice come out not apple or any other juice" just as whenever another squeezes us or in other words pushes our buttons and "whatever comes out is what is inside our self." So if anger comes out in our reaction then it's a limited automatic lower consciousness vibration from our subconscious memories. If instead we've practice and it's become natural and instead of anger coming out as in the past, compassion comes out then we are responding of a higher vibration. We continue to do that until we have squeezed out all old automatic reactions to high responses so it sustains our high vibration. And this does affect everything from our health and what we are manifesting or creating and how blissful our days really become, it affects everything.

I-M can Remind Us to Stay in the Present Moment ... To Create the Reality we Prefer

I-M is a reminder that the power is in the present moment of now and that we are always in the process of creating our reality and in the powerful present moment we can change it to create what we prefer. I-M can become a snap to be used as your reminder on a daily and hourly basis. When you come to know that whatever you put your attention upon will be what you are creating and it may become a passion for you too. You will want to be aware as much as you can to remind yourself. Because everything becomes easier and simpler on the infinite manifesting path and you become to know it is always up to you.

So just click your fingers to evolving your path of unfolding a perpetual flow of making the unknown known while creating days of bliss too. It really does feel like you have a magic wand and you do and the wand is your freedom to know you can choose the thoughts that you know is the reality you want to experience. It is easier then trying to change beliefs so that your reality can change to what you prefer it to be. To use an analogy of a video tape and having to go through the video tape by fast forwarding, rewinding until you find the part you want.

When we compare that to a DVD disc that you can choose from the list of chapters and you can go right to the chapter that you want. That would be the same with trying to keep track of old beliefs and trying to change them to new ones. Instead you can just keep thinking the new thoughts until they become the new belief. Then the belief that is created from the new thoughts becomes the reality. It became for me a domino effect that continues to unfold daily now to more powerful experiences.

Keeping a Journal of Your Experiences

Do you keep a journal of your experiences of the desires you have manifested? And a journal of all your desires and wants you still want to manifest. By adding to your journal every day is a great way to be a reminder for you of your wants and desires that have manifested. Whether the manifestations are small or big, they are all important when you are looking back whenever you may have a downer day. You know those off days when the old programs pop in without your noticing and then can take you into feeling hopeless instead of hopeful?

It can be exactly what you need to bring you back into the hope vibe and get you back on track with your creating process of manifesting. The trusting, knowing vibration that will boost you back up. With each manifestation you keep in your journal you can add how you felt before, during and after your manifestation. In the beginning this can be so worthwhile and so profound as reminders that we do create and affect all of our reality. Keeping you empowered instead of disempowered.

Sovereignty is the Way

CHAPTER 4

✳ ✳ ✳ ✳ ✳ ✳ ✳ ✳ ✳ ✳ ✳ ✳

INFINITE THOUGHTS

Infinite thought's is choosing from the infinite consciousness of all possibilities. The unlimited memories of thinking consciousness of All That Infinitely Is which means that anything and everything that we can imagine is possible.

There is no perception of linear thinking of time and space because that is breaking the infinite into linear perception of past, present and future like slides of a slide projector compared to a video. When we choose infinite thoughts and focus into the infinite manifesting mind we are going beyond social limited thinking consciousness of mind into the beyond which is infinitely of all dimensional realities. We are in no time, no space of all possibilities that consist of dimensions that we have not even imagined yet.

INFINITE MANIFESTING

Trying to grasp the Infinite is like trying to hold water in your hands because it is always in a flux of creating and manifesting from all dimensions. Especially trying to perceive it from a limited state of being mind limits it right from the get go. Even if we have expanded and evolved to comprehending it, it still will be elusive because infinite is forever.

Eternal, forever or infinite is such a challenge for us to comprehend because of our physical body's abilities and subconscious memories. Though we are evolving to know more of the infinite manifesting mind we are still limited when we are trying to perceive it from the body perspective.

We have to go beyond the body to knowing we are eternal beings to begin with, then we venture into the unknown territory. Continuously we then expand by choosing infinite thoughts that expands our mind of the eternal.

When we start to understand the concept of infinite consciousness, everything is occurring instantaneously, everything is going on all at once. We may still be trying to comprehend how everything is going on at once? Especially if it is from a limited perception of linear thinking, it may constrain us. When we choose infinite thoughts we work from comprehending no beginnings or endings, it will always expand our thoughts from our linear beliefs and take us into unknown mysteries to desire to know more.

This is where we our linear thoughts and beliefs become to crumble away because when we are focused in the infinite manifesting mind or infinite consciousness and are choosing infinite thoughts we are limitless and timelessly infinite. That is the reason we are able to experience what is referred to as beyond the ordinary to extraordinary. Beyond the normal into paranormal, beyond what seems impossible to the norm to experiencing many seeming mysterious things as no longer a mystery for us.

All of our old definitions that label our old beliefs no longer make any sense to us because we have evolved into understanding the mystery to know. All it took for me was to experience a few OOB experiences, to look down at my body to know that I was more then what I thought I was. Or to bend metal with my energy of intention without any physical force to realize that reality is more dream like. Compared to what my physical altered personality thinking of reality had once convinced me of it being so solid and fixed.

Infinite Thoughts to Ponder about our Dream Dimensional Reality

Just thinking about being in a dream and not awakening from it allowed me to realize how our senses can fool us into believing in the illusion of solidness when it is not. Choosing infinite thoughts allowed me to ponder about our dream dimensional reality. I wondered how I would know the difference. I would still be actively creating and living in my dream reality as if that was then my real physical life. This pondering created me to evolve into showing me what death really is just another dimensional reality and just as real as this reality we are living presently.

In the dream state of being we are doing everything we do in the reality we went to sleep from and actually more. We can fly, transform ourselves into others or anything, the possibilities are infinite. Now death takes on a whole other meaning for me as it did before and I realized that expanding to choosing infinite thoughts will lead us to expand and evolve further. To realize that life really is not as we think it is compared to the linear ego personality that is limited in social consciousness compared to infinite consciousness. It is only a tiny glimpse of the whole picture of reality.

When we compare it to a grain of sand on a beach that extends for miles upon miles this is similar to the infinite manifesting source that is expanding with each momentum in the hologram of all that is.

It does lead us to expand into seeing that many past illusion that we perceived as mysterious becomes less mysterious, like removing a layer bit by bit. Then our physical brain the receiving unit adapts the new information by re-wiring it for the infinite programs to run for our infinite experiences. It really is when we consciously, by being aware, choose infinite thoughts that it will expand our selves to know more and more.

Our Brain

We now know that we are using less then five percent of our brain, more or less depending on how evolved our states of being is. However, we know that there is a massive percentage left that is not activated that has potential for us to use. That is what going beyond limited thoughts to infinite thoughts can lead us. When we do come to realize that infinite thoughts lead to infinite abilities that are paranormal psychic experiences and do rewire our brain to activate more of our potential for us to experience. We change and evolve to use more or our power in each practice and experiences we have that goes beyond the ordinary ones. Then we become to naturally tune into our higher self that has always been there for us. Though it's not until we quiet the altered rational thinking so that we then get a clear signal to hear, feel or know clearly.

We always know the differences, it is quite extreme just as day is to night, the higher self guidance is always a heartfelt great feeling compared to the altered personality of the demanding emotionally addictive part of us.

Infinite manifesting from the infinite consciousness of all possibilities will always lead us ahead of the norm leaving tracks for others to follow as collective consciousness catches up in whatever reality we are in at any present moment. This is been ongoing forever and will continue to go on forever. This leads us to unity because we come to know that we are all one piece or flavor from the ONE SOURCE of infinite mind. Just as a hologram shows us that no matter what piece we cut out of the whole of it will also be contained in any and every piece we cut out. Each one of us is those pieces and together we make the holographic whole of the Infinite Source, the Infinite Mind of the Infinite Creator.

We then see through all the illusions especially the one that dictates our experiences to be seen as separate from everyone and thing. So consciously choosing from infinite thoughts and ideas from the infinite source leads us to evolve blissfully as we go.

Chapter 5

✳ ✳ ✳ ✳ ✳ ✳ ✳ ✳ ✳ ✳ ✳ ✳

INFINITE CREATORS

Being Infinite Creators we are able to own more and more of our power. We first must know that we are Infinite Creator's creating every single experience in our lives, because without that awareness we are creating our life through illusions. Illusions give the appearance that everything just happens to us, whether it is our health, our jobs, our incomes, our relationships, our families and friends and interactions. Especially when we experience anything we do not like and give our power away to the lower vibrations of frequencies of hate, blame, revenge which is all judgments of our experiences. We can see the difference between an finite creator creating compared to an infinite creators creations.

Infinite Creators See through Illusions

As Infinite Creators we know through our experiences that we are the creator's of our reality by the thoughts we are choosing, whether aware or not, those thoughts are creating our reality all day long. When we get to the knowing that this is the way it is and has always been and will always be then we take our power back and see through all the illusions.

It would be the same way that a magician can trick us to believe that a magic trick they perform is real until we are shown how to do the magic trick for our self. When we know how the trick is played we then have the power also to perform it, we are no longer the audience watching and being tricked. Just like being in the audience of our life instead of being the magician and knowing how reality really works.

We then become to realize that all of the power comes in the knowledge of the knowing of its truth, we are infinite creators creating our reality and when we know it we then can take responsibility for our reality. To know what we are thinking and talking about is creating reality all day long and creating our future by its momentum. By knowing that gives us so much power because we are then living a life deliberately leaving nothing to chance or on automatic reactions. As infinite creators consciously we choose our creations consciously.

We leave nothing to chance

When we get to this point of evolving we then know that everything and every interaction and experience is creating by our own self. There is no randomness of things ever just happening to us, everything is now observed as our own creations, whether they are negative or positive creations. All creations are a result of our own thinking and to see the feedback of your own proof is to observe to see how it is always thoughts you thought and or talked about that came about in your experiences. When we observe long enough we will see our own proof and there will be no denying that each of us is creating our reality all day long and our future too. So that everything we see is a self reflection that will always show us feedback.

Observing our self and everything that is occurring within our days will show us how we are creating our life. Then we evolve to realizing that webbed into our observing is actually creating how we observe as quantum physics now proves through all of the experiments that have been done. We as observers affecting our reality by how we observe it. So it is a two fold benefit because by observing we are realizing by our own feedback of proof that our thoughts are creating our reality. The way we observe our reality is the actuality of how our reality unfolds and is affected by our observations of it.

Using our Power as the Observer

I have found that the more I practice anything for a few weeks by observing anything in any new way compared to the past old ways, the new ways become just as automatic and natural as the old way was. Then all my old reactions are no longer automatic and the new responses are the automatic way I respond to anything that triggered me before and that changes everything. All these newer ways are the infinite creator's way to respond. Knowing we are the observer affecting all situations in a better way then we have done in the past changes the affect of how our reality unfolds in its creation.

As we experience to notice more and more proof for our self then we are inspired to continue the new changes. By observing everything with our awareness because we now know that it is the way we are observing and responding to everything that is continuously creating our reality. We then choose to observe and respond in the most positive or loving way because of our wisdom from the knowledge of our experiences. Responding to others as we would choose them to respond to our self takes on a whole new meaning.

We are Multidimensional Beings

As infinite creators we become to know that we are multidimensional beings, there is more to us then what just appears in the objective physical reality we perceive. There is also more to us then just our physical body. When we expand and open our minds to evolved knowledge, we can tune into these other dimensions through our imagination.

Our mind through our powerful imagination is where we are focused upon even though our body may be stationary in one physical place. Just as you are sitting probably on a chair and reading your mind is not always focused on your physical body. It is focused on what you are reading or other thoughts that are passing by through your mind.

As you sit on your chair you can expand your thoughts to be so focused on a friend for a period of time. For that period of time it could be that you are really intertwined and entangled with your friend through imagination. As your body sits in the chair you can focus your imagination to be anywhere of any distance away from your body's focused thoughts upon it.

Just as when we fall asleep and dream and you are focused in that dimensional reality experiencing everything as real until you awake back into being focused in your objective physical reality again.

When we realized as infinite creators we are more then our physical senses show us that we are dimensional beings always traveling without our body as we travel with our focused thoughts it can be powerful awakening and adventurous journey

Life Becomes Blissful

Knowing we are Creator's we no longer deny or doubt that we create our reality and every part of it. Then we pull all of our power back to our self because no one can alter our thoughts that we are choosing to create from. Doing it blissfully means that through our awareness of how we observe everything becomes how we respond. It is when we respond and it becomes natural in the most blissful ways because that is what we will be continuously creating. Then we are choosing from the infinite source of manifesting. We become to enjoy blissful experiences and the creations of them through our observing and creating. All challenges become opportunity for evolving growth in every part of our life.

Then what we will become to notice is that any type of depression fades away because depression is only a result from thoughts that create feelings of hopelessness. And that comes from thoughts that create the feelings that we do not have any control or power to change anything in our life. When we know we can by owning our creating abilities and creations as a result then we are empowered. We know we are the infinite creators creating our life by how we observe and respond to everything, we take our power back from the illusions that once distorted our thoughts about life.

We know we are the infinite creators in being and can change our thoughts always to what we prefer to experience in all our creations. Our life becomes a joyful exuberant experience daily and the momentum expands into everything we perceive. We know that we are what we think we are and experience it all the time now. We own our infinite creator abilities because our experiences will always be our feedback of proof that confirms it to our self. We then live our life as infinite creators by how we now think and that thinking creates the most powerful feelings. Infinite Creators choose Infinite Thoughts to create all we desire from all possibilities into manifestations.

Higher Self

Higher Self is just one label, just like everything else there are so many varieties of label's for everything that really means the same. Some refer to the Holy Spirit, Natural Self, Source,, Jesus, God, Future Self, Entities, Soul and so on. However, names are only invented labels to define something through verbal language so we can give reference to when verbally communicating. If we are a part of One Infinite Source and beyond any illusion we are One, unified, we don't need labels.

Since we still need to use labels I will be using the label Higher or Infinite Self when describing the larger part of our selves. Just as the majority of the population goes through so many stages in the first 30 years of our physical lives, most of us are not paying much attention to our higher self or any communication on a conscious level. Though we are guided but usually the altered ego personality takes the lead in guiding us to make our choices. However for the exceptions it can be the opposite as psychic, indigo, light children and so on are consciously connected right from birth. If we do not stay aware then we eventually loose the communication or conscious connection somewhere along our physical developing stages. Or most do not tune in until we have passed those developing stages of growth until later on. Or it is when we set the time aside to pray or meditate which for many is not that often or very long periods during our day.

So praying or meditating is still using a connection to communicate to or through a higher power or source, whether it is a God or Jesus or

Saint or whatever the Source is. It can again all be refer to a Higher Source.

A Trip Down Memory Lane

For myself I used prayer throughout my first 30 years, praying to God mostly and then near the end tried to listen, however it was usually before going to sleep at night or when I needed to ask for something really important in my life. I read that prayer is asking the question and meditation is the listening part of the communication to a higher source. This made sense to me as I was raised Catholic with an Anglican mix, so at first I did what most Catholic's do go to church and did my confessions to a priest. Then the priest would give me my sentence, oops, Freudian slip there, I mean penance.

Until I went to a Ukrainian school and was taught to do my confession as we all sat in the church pews and confessed by our self. It was a one on one communication, no more middle man, so I could confess to the supreme higher being, God without a medium to interpret for me. That was great! I really liked that much better and it was from then on that I stopped going to the confession booth. Just a quick chuckle I must add in here, I read not long ago that in some country they are now using a phone booth to confess sins to the priest.

The Ukrainian school created a shift or a change for me and it was my beginning of taking more of my power back allowing me to speak or think, communicate to the Higher Source which at that time I still referred to as God. Now I refer to God as a Creator or Infinite Intelligence, again it is all the same thing with different labels, One Infinite Source.

It was not until I was a teenager that my mother allowed me to no longer go to church. I don't know what took her so long for that permission to be granted to me because my dad was the Ukrainian

Anglican and he never had to go to church. So now no more church and I could just confess my sins to God and sit and listen to the answers. Sometimes I was on the right path of hearing my higher self other times I was listening to my personality ego, back then I did not realize there was a difference. Except the Catholic religion labeled sin and the devil as most of us now label it as ego and higher source.

Back To The Present

To speed up the history here, now I do know the difference, just as you who are reading this probably do and probably went through similar experiences to get to where you are now. Now I know there is Infinite Consciousness which I think is the Mind of God or Creator and we are all waving along with our experiences of creating our realities kind of like being in the Creators dream from different channeled frequency's of the Creator's one source mind. And just as all of us can have empathetic feelings for anything our children or family members go through, the Creator may also. However we also give our children free will when they are on they're own, we can guide them with some of our own wisdom however they do have their own free will and choices to make for their learning experiences. Just as what may be going on with the Creator and our lives, realities we are creating and experiencing.

Our Own Higher Self Is Like Our Soul Mate

For myself I get the feeling that our physical body is still not attainable to carry or frequenize the whole of us, so just a small part of our whole comes into our physical body. Just like quantum mechanics and the wave/particle duality interpretation. And is the reason I think that the other part of our self could really be the first and most important label to define our soulmate. It's such an uplifted and self love feeling and it then becomes so natural without any conditions. Our soulmate or higher self is connected to All That Is, Creator. Our higher self knows everything about our self and knows everything simultaneously removed of time and space while we are in such linear perception.

To use an example of our higher self being like the eagle and our physical self to be the mouse. We can realize through this analogy of an example how our higher self then can know everything and is the best guide for us to follow in guidance of our purposeful soul path. I found through my own experiences and being self aware through practicing I became to know the difference between my higher self and my ego or chattering thoughts or memories. When we become this aware of the differences then we become to live each day clearly from our higher self's guidance. Life really does change and in the most amazing ways.

Once we come to realize what all the Master Teachers have taught that by following of our bliss, excitement, joy, love, all the really good great feelings. By now we have learned all about the EGO and how it likes to direct us by fearful doubtful ways. Until our ego will merge more and more, the more that we be empathetic with compassion to it in the most loving way. It still is amazing to me how we separate the whole of ourselves but it is the process we go through as we evolve. Higher self leads us to evolve to become infinite creators. The further along that we evolve we then get to realize and know that all of these seeming separate parts of ourselves are just like looking at a tree without seeing all the roots below the ground. Or the analogy of only seeing the tip of an iceberg above the water when we look below the water we then see the biggest past of the iceberg, just as our physical self is like the top above the water and the rest of our whole self is below the water.

So for me my higher self is my soul mate, or to use the famous saying, "the other half" of me. Any other being is secondary when it comes to my guidance. It is my choice not to alter from my higher self because it does know everything that I ever need to know.

So Who Knows What Is best For Our Self? Our Higher Self!

Who should we always turn to? Our Higher Self!

What is becoming an evolving sovereign being? Merging our ego and higher self lovingly!

How do we know we are picking up higher self information? We will know by following our joy, excitement, bliss, peace, unconditional love and passion.

It is the most simplistic way to know not only what direction you are heading but also the most powerful knowing information that will always lead you in the right direction, step by step by following your highest vibration feelings.

CHAPTER 6

* * * * * * * * * * * *

OBSERVER EFFECT

We are the observer affecting it all, everything, it's our nature and the nature of reality. Yet do not let the assumption of observing be perceived as non action ability because thinking and observing are so intertwined. It is the thoughts that we use while observing, in quantum mechanics it is labeled the observer effect. Even if we are in a conversation with another and the other person is talking and we are listening, through our listening we are still observing because thoughts are on going.

Observing the Hawk

I'd like to share an experience I had this morning as it may also spark your own observer effect too. I took a walk outside and watched a hawk flying in the sky then the hawk started to circle around in one spot. As I continued to observe the hawk it took a slow dive down to the ground. Now this can be important for you too as it was for me. As you read the sentence of the hawk slowly diving to the ground what was your first impression or thought? The more honest you are with your own self the better the realization will be.

Did you think, "It was going down for some food" or "poor mouse or animal on the ground?" What was your first thought? Was it from a victim observer thinking? Or maybe you were thinking what it would be like to be a hawk flying above?

Since we are affecting our reality by how we observe it this can be very enlightening for our selves. The hawk could have been diving down for a hamburger someone threw away or something other then a live prey.

What the hawk did is not as important as how our first thoughts were in interpreting the situation we observed.

This is how easily we can get into practicing the **observer effect** throughout our day, first by noticing and being self aware. And then to changing our thoughts when we do take notice.

Letting Go of Self Judgments

It is really powerful to keep in mind that it is not wise to judge our self because the observer is still affecting our reality. If your first impression was perceived as victim thoughts do not judge yourself in any negative way because that will only lead to perpetual fear thoughts, yes into more victimizing of your self.

It is noticing the first thoughts of impression that is empowering because that will lead into becoming an aware observer. It is by noticing and then working on changing the choices of thoughts for the next time and the next time. Until it becomes habitual to be aware and changing it to a non victim perception instead of the automatic thinking that usually takes over without any noticing. It is that automatic thinking that continuously creates our day and life to be either what we want or what we don't want. The way we observe everything will always be up to our own self.

Remember the observer effect is going on all the time and we can change everything when we practice observing deliberately by noticing our thoughts. The thoughts we put the most attention on that becomes what we believe about everything. Just as quantum experiments show the proof that we are collapsing the wave of potential possibilities by the way we observe.

It will be the affect as the wave collapses into a physical particle of reality, the reality we then experience.

When Everything Starts to Fall Apart Get Excited!

Why? We're under Construction

Knowing our self as the observer affecting our reality changes everything when we realize what is going on behind the illusions of everything falling apart in our lives. No matter what area it is in your life or every area of you life, remind yourself that everything needs to fall apart before it can restructure itself back together again. We, the observer are affecting reality by how we perceive everything that falls apart.

It reminds me of the nursery rhyme,
"Humpty dumpty sat on a wall
Humpy dumpty had a great fall
All the kings' horses and all the kings' men
Couldn't put humpty together again."

When we perceive it through wisdom of our own experiences it can have a powerful shift in what goes on when our life seems to fall apart! My interpretation of the rhyme is humpty dumpty is similar to our old beliefs falling apart for the new beliefs to take form. When we desire to create a new reality, of course the old beliefs are not going to be what creates the new reality. It could be the reasoning that all the kings men could not put humpty back together again. As our old beliefs are falling apart it makes sense that everything in our lives will also fall apart too.

Let's use an example of my job becoming redundant after 19 years of working at it. I had new desires but I didn't take any action to allow my new desires to manifest because I didn't take action to leave with my own free will. Though I did give a lot of attention on thoughts about not working at my job quite often, many times without realizing it till I seen it through hindsight. At the time it was my fear beliefs that stopped me in taking any action but my thoughts of not working was already in the process of manifesting, as it did manifest. I was still hanging on to my desire simultaneously and without taking any action and my desire did become manifested. It appeared as an illusion that I had nothing to do with it however I had everything to do with it. I was the observer affecting my own reality by how I was observing through my thought process.

No longer having my job was a very big structure for my life at that time, my income and job really became my life's priority and webbed out into everything else in my life. This was the reason I stayed at my job longer and in the fear mode without taking physical action myself.

During a couple of years when I had the desire to quit work but did not quit, I did become sick with migraines and had frequent colds and illnesses. Even at the time I knew what was going on in my body and mind connection. I allowed the fear thoughts to take over and blocked the energy for my desire to manifest quicker. It was the fear that created my immune system to start to break down by not taking action, it was in disharmony. It was more proof for me to realize how I was affecting my life and body. Also how detrimental fear can be on our body and our life if we do not change our fear thoughts to love (potential) thoughts.

It also appears that it can be the most depressing, out of control experience that can happen to someone, yet behind the illusion of random occurrences I knew what was going on. I could see where it was all heading if I did not change my choice of thoughts, so I did!

Knowing that I do create all of my reality and that the observer effect is always going on I perceived it as a celebration of excitement instead of in fear. This did change everything because my migraines disappeared and so did the colds and illness. It was a double win experience because letting go of the fear and instead choosing better thoughts allowed my body to respond back to its natural well being. And my new life could also now unfold. I know that if I did not change my thoughts then the little illnesses would transform into disease at some point. This is what self healing is all about.

Receiving a Gift is More Exciting When We Open It

So we can see the reason that everything does have to fall apart before it comes back together in another new way for our desire to be fulfilled into manifestation. We could use an analogy of receiving a gift and the gift being our reality of our life that is under construction. We can guess and assume but until we open the wrapped gift will be when we know what is inside of it.

So that is the reason it's of our most powerful benefit to perceive all experiences in our life that may seem so disastrous or appearing as random situations to be perceived with awareness and excitement. As it will leads us to continue to create our life the quantum way by paying attention how we as the observer are affecting our lives by the THOUGHTS we choose to use, making then infinite thoughts lead to an empowering life.

Chapter 7

✱ ✱ ✱ ✱ ✱ ✱ ✱ ✱ ✱ ✱ ✱ ✱

APPRECIATION

COUNT YOUR BLESSINGS & YOUR LIFE WILL CHANGE IN MAGICAL WAYS

Count your blessings instead of sheep is a song in the movie "White Christmas" and has been a catalyst for me in being gratefully appreciative for everything, yes even the so called judged negative experiences too.

The song's lyrics is about count your blessings instead of the old way of counting sheep to allow one to fall asleep easily. However counting sheep was not something I have ever done to fall asleep. Even a couple decades ago, before my awakening to all of this wisdom

I did allow worry thoughts to NOT put me to sleep. I would toss and turn for hours. So the metaphor for counting sheep can be to realize that being too focused on our worries, which is expanding on fearful thoughts. And that is not what any of us want

Hindsight Leads the Way

In hindsight I can see how critical that actually was for myself and my body and daily reality that became from doing that because I did not know what I know now. I can now see exactly how my reality became unfolded into manifested stormy experiences. Thoughts matter and I kept focusing on what I did not want without realizing what I was creating as a result.

It was an old automatic way of thinking, pessimistically from addictive emotions that kept me spinning the same web.

I was sick all of the time with many illnesses which is completely opposite of how my body and life is now. Just from choosing better thoughts and appreciating instead of fear based thinking.

Now I fall asleep thinking about my desires already manifested and how I would be living them, which is the energy thoughts to the desires becoming manifested. Which I continue to do to this day. You may also find this too that when you start to visualize the good thoughts you fall asleep so quickly.

It makes all the difference not only in how my daily life is created or shifted and becomes the way I desire it and my sleep and dreams and when I awake. You will notice that your dreams are happier and quite amazing and when you awake you will feel so refreshed and actually excited to get on with your day. Your day will become what you always desired it to be.

My Sister's Idea Seeded and Transformed Appreciation to Become Natural of a Great New Habit

With the added benefit that my sister came up with years ago of a Gratitude List. Every week we send an email of the things we gratefully appreciate to share with each other. With the intention of a reminder that can sometimes can go unnoticed in our daily living. By sharing it for years, it expanded our selves to amazing powerful ways to have it become a natural thing to do all day, every day, a great habit.

Of course the powerful benefits to count your blessings of appreciation is how it expands and changes how you feel on a daily basis while simultaneously creating your desires to manifest more easily and naturally. Counting your blessings then becomes your experiences each day especially when it becomes so natural that you do not have to remind your self to do it because it becomes automatic. And that is the state of being we will become to be and our thoughts will also be of that too.

What about the Negative Things To Count Your Blessings For?

Now that I can automatically appreciate, as it has become a great habit, anything, person or situation becomes my mirror reflection that shows me what I need to work on for myself. Anything that I judge negative quickly transforms to my opportunity to shift to actually appreciate the situation or experience.

Count your blessings often and it will quickly change your perception of it too.

So count your blessings and watch how your life will transform to experiencing your creations daily the way you desire them to be manifested. Magically and miraculously your day will amaze you at being the way you want it to be.

When you count your blessings it helps in letting go with the magical dusting of grateful appreciation. Even the habit of trusting, which is what letting go is all about so that you can allow your desires to manifest easily. It is all connected so infinite intelligently.

So count your blessings, you are infinitely worth it! When you really start to appreciate yourself, which means being aware that you do appreciate things about your self and all that you are. You become to love and accept yourself for the Divine Being that You are in the Divine Creator's Creations of All That Is. Allowing all judgments to no longer be a part of your perception.

CHAPTER 8

✷ ✷ ✷ ✷ ✷ ✷ ✷ ✷ ✷ ✷ ✷ ✷

YOUR FIRST AWAKENING THOUGHTS

We know that thoughts are energy and we need to continue to remind ourselves that our thoughts really do matter and are creating reality.

When you awoke this morning, how did you feel? If you were rushed that created the feelings of a state of being uneasy, a flood of chemical reactions that flooded through your brain and body that created the feelings. That was all as a result of the rushed thinking that you awoke to and started to think about. When we become to know how the body and brain does work, we then can empower ourselves by creating our day our way and be the one in control. Instead of allowing automatic reactions to continue from some non potential thoughts that can run our day on automatic pilot from not being aware of what's going on.

If we wake up from our sleep rushed then we can stop in the midst of our thinking and CHOOSE different thoughts. By stopping the non potential thinking that we started our day with, we can change the chemical reactions that are firing the signals from our brain to our body cells. Changing the rushed feeling to a relaxed in control choice of thinking then relaxes our brain and body to a better state of being, removed of stress. It will reflect in other experiences we have that unfolds during our day as long as we continue the better thinking thoughts to choose from.

Choose Empowering Thoughts to Become a Habit

Creating a new habit takes some practice and the more we practice doing it the easier it will become. Take notice how you awake in the morning! If it is anything other then feeling good, then take it as a sign to stop the thinking you are choosing and choose better feeling thinking. It will create the difference in your day. Remind yourself that what you are thinking about is creating the next experience and then the next and so on.

Whenever you are not feeling good take that as a communication or a sign to change the path of your day. It will always come back to CHOOSING BETTER FEELING THINKING over not feeling good thinking. The choice will always be up to you, no one else, no matter what the situation or experience is that you find yourself in. It will always be up to your own self how you will respond to everything. The more that you continue to notice and choose better thinking you will create better and better experiences throughout your day.

What Emotions are You Addicted To?

We may not even notice until we have the knowledge that teaches us that we are addicted to certain emotions. If we get angry easily then we can change that addiction to becoming blissful naturally instead of angry.

How? By taking notice first and then changing our reactions as many times as we possibly can. Realize that the other individual or situation is only an opportunity to clean our own perception from fear energy to love energy. It may sound uncomfortable as first, however if done with consistency you will **think** the difference into **feeling** the difference every time you do it.

Knowing that any negative feelings you are experiencing is a chemical reaction to old ways that you have automatically reacted to in the past. It becomes a high, like a fix to get another high from habitual reactions of your past.

In the great movie "What the Bleep Do We Know" they talk about thoughts, the brain, the observer and to create the day we want. Let's use the example of driving along in your car and someone cuts you off and you have to move into the other lane of traffic. What was your first reaction? Was it anger? Remember under the illusion of anger is fear. Your reaction to fear of getting in an accident triggered the chemical reaction to react in anger and blame of the other driver.

Do you curse the other driver? Or have you gone a step beyond and ask yourself how did my thoughts create my vibration of energy to be in this destiny moment of this experience?

These two questions make all the difference in how you will change the chemical reactions in your brain and body for the next unfolding experiences you create.

When we realize that many of our reactions are a result from the thoughts we have been choosing without awareness, which means automatically then we can choose different thoughts. The different thoughts will then create better experiences. Until we create it to be a habit through our awareness that will be the changes we will see, the better experiences being created into our experiences.

To break the old addictions of disempowering thinking is to be aware and choose better potential ways of thinking that will create the better experiences. Our thoughts we are choosing are that energetic and will be the only way to change our reality.

To become addicted to the good feeling thinking will then become habitual and through practice will become as natural as the old fear reactions were originally. All it takes is awareness throughout the day on how you are feeling because we can only feel what we were thinking about first.

Reminding our self that the thinking we are doing is creating all of our reality and as we change the choice of our thinking we will be experiencing the changes in our reality as we are creating it. Our words will also start to change. By noticing how our words change from fear energy words to better feeling words all from our choice of thoughts will become to appear magically. Yet we know that it's a result from all the great work we have done on a conscious level by being aware and making the choice of thinking the way we prefer.

CHAPTER 9

* * * * * * * * * * * * *

FINITE AND INFINITE CREATIONS

Infinite creations are created from infinite consciousness which is unlimited with no beginnings or endings compared to finite realities that have beginnings and endings. Finite creations of consciousness are thoughts that consist of waves of thoughts from the limited constricted conglomeration wavelengths. By limited I mean the ordinary continuous momentum of normal everyday reality that the majority are choosing thoughts from. Finite is limited because it has a beginning and ending as in our linear perceptional reality that we perceive as a time line of past, present and future.

When we are stuck in finite thoughts of thinking and creating we are limited because we are either thinking in of our past or of our future. If we continue that way it takes away most of our power because the present moment is where all the power really is and where we are creating all of the time.

The Power is in the Present and Simultaneously Creating your Reality. We are always creating from the POWERFUL PRESENT

It is so powerful whether we **are aware** or **not aware** of it, it is still the force that is creating dependant on what we are focusing upon through our thoughts. And when we are aware how and what we are focused upon in the present moment we become more powerful because we can be conscious of what we choose to focus upon. We can be the deliberate conscious creator creating from the infinite thoughts. The creator who is choosing the reality that we want to be living compared to living what we do not want.

To check it out you can do it right now, this moment as you are reading this, ask yourself? Are you totally focused on what you are reading? Or are you thinking about something in the past that happened or thinking about something in the future?

This can be quite the exuberant realization because we so easily change to what we are focusing upon without realizing it. So when you are reading this your thoughts can easily drift to something that happened this morning or what you should make for dinner tonight. Or anything else that your attention is not on instead of being focused in what you are presently intending to be focused upon. What is really amazing is the aware realization that in each present moment we are actually in a state of flux of creating all day long by what we are putting our attention and focus upon.

Though we may not be able to keep track of all the thoughts we choose and then focus upon through out every day because it is always on going, however we can choose to be aware as much as we can. This then creates it to be a habit of being aware instead of not being aware. This does make all the difference if we you want to be creating what you want instead of what you do not want. The **knowing awareness** that we are creating moment by moment in our present gives us the power to continuously be more aware and redirect our thoughts so that we continue to create only what we do want.

Choosing our thoughts of Present Focusing of Attention

It is when we are reminding our self throughout the day that it will become natural and habitual the more that we do it. That means being aware and bringing our thoughts back to what we are actually doing in each moment that we are aware of it. So when you are reading then your thoughts stay focused on what you are reading about. When you keep your thoughts focused on what you are really thinking and doing you are in the powerful present moment. No matter what you are doing it is practicing to be aware of what you are thinking about. Then you are aware if it is in alignment with any outcome you want to have manifested.

Finite thinking is creating from the present by putting attention in limited ways by thinking in any fearful, doubtful, hopeless ways.

Let us use an example of wanting to play the piano. The finite limited thoughts would go like this, oh how I would love to play the piano, but it would take so much practice and I do not think I would be able to do it. That is already setting your self up in a limited way to create because it is choosing from the limited finite consciousness. If you changed your thoughts to think, I know I could do it I just have to keep practicing and then by practicing I would eventually be able to play some songs. This is a bit better of a vibration to think from however it is still finite and limited because it still is creating from the limits of practicing.

Now if you were to think from the **infinite thoughts** then your thoughts would be more like this, I would love to play the piano, and I know that if I put my attention into focusing on already playing the piano with such perfection then I would link into that reality that is already going on.

The differences is so powerful because when we choose the infinite thinking we are bypassing all limits and time to use our ability in the most profound ways. There would be no practicing. Instead we would use our imagination in the most infinite ways by already tapping into a reality of another who plays piano with such perfection. We then instantly tapped into that reality and become a channel or linked to that reality then we open our self to receive that energy. Then our experience would seem so magical or miraculously to others because we would sit down at a piano and just play beautifully.

There are individuals doing that now. Burt Goldman the creator of "Quantum Jumping" teaches how to tap in by quantum jumping to receive the information we need. He heals others and has become an artist by quantum jumping. His beautiful artistic painting ability flows through from another reality, another multidimensional self. That is infinite manifesting from the infinite source.

Nicole Whitney the creator and the host of "News for the Soul" talk radio does the same thing when she sits at a piano. She naturally becomes in the same frequency of consciousness flow of another entity's energy to come through her and then plays beautiful songs. Though she has never played the piano before she has tuned into the infinite manifesting source and it flows out of her. She also teaches spoon bending that I learned from her course, which is the same infinite source we go to when bending or twisting spoons or any metal. It is the same source we go to by focusing on anything when we are in concentration or meditation.

I do it all the time with my writing by quieting my mind and focusing on allowing information to flow out and then it does. It is going into the infinite manifesting source that is open to infinite information and infinite dimensions. Instead of only tapping into to the finite source of consciousness that is limited and instead go to the extraordinary experiences of realities, infinite consciousness.

Beliefs Change along the Way from Finite Thoughts to Infinite Thoughts

We do not have to be concerned about our old beliefs because when we continue to choose from infinite thoughts then our beliefs naturally change. They change to accommodate from the new infinite experiences and infinite creations we are having. Before you even realize it your beliefs are changed. So remember all is possible when we choose thoughts from the infinite vibration of frequencies compared to the finite.

Chapter 10

✳ ✳ ✳ ✳ ✳ ✳ ✳ ✳ ✳ ✳ ✳ ✳

EGO OR INFINITE BEING

Our ego is the collection of memories that we have stored in our subconscious and is finite in dimension of consciousness. When we consider when we keep our focus whether aware of it or not in that lower memories we then access into social consciousness. Social consciousness is the finite dimension of continuous thoughts of lower vibration frequencies from every being infinitely that we perpetually recycle and use.

Ego ... Low Vibrations Consciousness

Fear, guilt, hate, despair, doubt, hopelessness, pessimism, judging, blame, revenge, anger, hurt, sadness, separation, depression and so on. So when we entertain those lower vibrations for any length of time we are then being influenced by our ego or subconscious memories of data. It's the doorway that leads to infinite rooms or dimensions of similar thoughts and it can go on endlessly through the lower vibrations of consciousness.

Our ego was designed when we come into our physical embodiment for the purpose of allowing us to be aware, to keep us out of danger, alert us so that we can keep our of harms way sort of thing. However it became engrossed as through human history with all the conditioning of fear. Fear became a way to keep the mass population in control in many instances. We all can realize that when we use fear tactics we then have the ability to control another if the other is living from those lower dimensions of thoughts and beliefs. The simplest thing to know is to perceive ego as low vibration collection of memories of consciousness compared to infinite being as a higher vibration.

Infinite Being ... Higher Vibration Frequencies

When we come to the realization that our body is only a vehicle for our infinite being or source then we can easily grasp it all in a bigger picture of what reality is. Our infinite being, our connection to the Source of All That Is, God, Universe, whatever label you may use is All That Is and is infinitely expanding.

So our Infinite Being will influence to lead us in directions that will be for our higher purpose or highest good, however from our ego's perception many times it just may not make sense. Yet if we go by how we feel it makes it much simpler and easier. Our Infinite Being is not bound to linear physical dimensions as our physical brain or body is, it sees beyond into infinity, into all past, present and future, so it is the best guider for us. It's the old lower programs that separates us from our infinite being, once we realize that we can easily by awareness and observation connect or be guided much easier.

Infinite Being ... Higher Vibration Consciousness

Love, hopeful, optimism, trust, acceptance, uplifted, excitement, blissful, knowing surpassing believing, expecting the best becomes normal, empathy and passion and so on. It sure is quite the differences of feelings from lower to higher vibrations.

Using a Pane of Glass as an Analogy of Illusions of our Infinite Being v/s Ego

Our infinite being is never really separated except through the illusion that it is which our old programs that seem to continue to convince or trick us into the illusions. Using the analogy of a pane of glass just came to my mind to use. When silver is applied to one side of a pane of glass then we only see our reflection, however if there is no silver applied to the glass then it's a window that we can see through.

Illusion can be like the glass, whether with silver applied or no silver. If we are guided mostly by our ego then we only see reflections of consciousness like the glass with the silver lining that gives us a reflection back to us as limited social consciousness dimension. But if we remove that silver so that it is just a plain glass window to see through, in other words remove the illusions of separation then we see through it and can perceive more of what's really going on, what other dimensions are available to us.

By merging the ego bit by bit so that it becomes more comfortable with the whole of it all, we are dissolving the silver bit by bit. It's like the kundalini experience, bit by bit it becomes easier and comfortable however to open it up all at once will be quite a challenging uncomfortable experience. I have experienced it and if you have too then you know that the slower process of its unfolding is the easier to go through.

So how do we Become to know the Difference from our Ego's Guidance Compared to our Infinite Being Guidance?

Simply How We Feel is always our own indication of what vibration we are on or heading towards. If we don't feel very good then we've been allowing our old programs to influence us, whether we are aware or not, it's the way it seems to become. Being aware really does make all the difference.

If you find it a challenge in getting to better feelings it's only because you created it to be a habit to feeling down or lower frequencies of emotions. Practice again is what it takes to make it a habit. Especially when we are more habitual to be guided by our automatic old programs or emotional addictions for such a long time because blissful feeling may feel uncomfortable at first.

If we are feeling good, then we are being influenced by our infinite being. Every master teacher teaches feeling good is our best indication of our Source or infinite spiritual self. That really does make it so much simpler then trying to weed everything out or trying to be aware of our thoughts all the time. Just by noticing how we are feeling in any moment shines the light on what we were thinking about and is the awareness and opportunity to then change how we feel by thinking better thoughts.

I love the way Bruce Lipton explains it that we can't be in protection and growth at the same time. Protection can be referred to as the ego and growth can be referred to as the infinite being.

Chapter 11

✳ ✳ ✳ ✳ ✳ ✳ ✳ ✳ ✳ ✳ ✳ ✳

POWERFUL PURPOSES IN CHALLENGES

Before we dive into what your powerful purpose is in any challenges you are going through, let's take a closer look at what beliefs may be attached to some words that define your ideas of the words you use most often.

I am quite sure by now you have already realized and transformed your perception, attitudes and beliefs of problems into challenges. If you have not, then this realization is this first step to change or transform your energy of what is attached to your beliefs. Once you perceive problems as challenges they become to hold less heaviness and negativity that perceiving problems contain as energy. Though challenges are a step up, it's still empowering to realize that even challenges can have a lower vibration. It is still attached with negative energy depending on our own beliefs.

If challenges still hold a lower vibration in your beliefs then what is actually being picked up in the tuning process is the belief that whatever you are going through is hard. Which defines it as a belief of not really possible or going to take a lot of work to get past your challenges. That is not the energy of vibration we want to continue with for any want or desires to manifest.

To get beyond the energy of problems transformed to challenges we still need to transform our challenges to see what our powerful purpose will be. We will find the answers of many questions in our purpose that is contained in our challenges to begin with. When we stop using the words problems, challenges and raise the words to higher vibrations as infinite words. Infinite words will expand into our powerful purpose so we can then perceive problems and challenges with a purpose. The feedback it shows is that by continuing to use problem and challenges to define your idea's of reality will also be more of the reality you will be creating.

Are you getting a WALA moment? I hope so! If not you will! Or maybe you already have figured this out, then congrats to you, big time, because that's what is needed to get to the next level of higher vibrations.

Reminding yourself that words do matter because they are energy too, they are the end result of your beliefs to show you your own feedback. It's so powerful to change the words you use regularly so that you are in a state of being of your most powerful potentials when it comes to manifesting what you want.

So when we really get it we then realize how important it is to change our use of words. No more seeing things or speaking of our problems or challenges because we have NOW transformed that old energy and are using words as **Powerful Purpose** instead.

For example let's say you have financial problems or challenges right now for many it's so automatic to think and talk about the challenge, Yet that's what keeps the problem of challenge to continue to create more problems or challenges. Instead whenever you talk or think about them, think or say, **I have a powerful purpose right now!** Do you feel the difference in how your emotions transforms into feelings of higher vibrations? And that is what will change to create the reality you prefer.

So the purpose of your challenge is the realization that leads you to know this information and change your words to higher vibration words for creating in higher vibrations. Without finding and working on the purpose you would become stuck in the problem and challenges.

Your Challenges Hold the Greatest Powerful Purpose Right Now

Now that we have taken our challenges to the next level, going beyond and transformed it into what may be our greatest powerful purpose. And that purpose may also be exactly what is needed to realize your guidance from your infinite self. That guidance may also be exactly what is needed to manifest your desires if we take a look at it from the future by using our imagination or mental visioning.

You can do this right now, a simple exercise, are you ready?

Whatever your challenge, just think about it…now think and envision it as the challenge you're having is resolved, whatever excitedly first comes to mind go with that! Now you are seeing it from the end and working from the end backwards. Do you see your resolved situation already accomplished? When you do and now by looking backwards you will see that the challenges that you were going through was exactly what you needed to begin with. Without that challenge you would not resolve it. Since you have done it mentally, now you can insert it by giving it more and more attention throughout your day. Because you know that eventually, depending on how much energy and emotion you give your vision resolved will be how quickly it will manifest in physical for you.

This is how you transform all challenges to see the silver lining of the powerful purpose it has for you. Every single challenge you have is lined or contains a powerful purpose and the challenge is only a stepping stone to your manifestation.

Our You Still Getting Stuck in Your Challenges

If you find that you have become stuck in your challenges then becoming aware that you are stuck of course is the first step to getting unstuck. When you realize you have become stuck, all it takes is realizing what powerful purpose it holds and that powerful purpose is the fuel, the leverage to pull you out of it. Realizing your powerful purpose will lift you up high enough to see all that was going on that was holding you back.

Things like forgetting throughout the day, not being aware of the words you are using, the thoughts you've been focusing upon, the visions you've been entertaining. Maybe even the negative emotional addiction you entangled with another in conversation, they are all energy that has been adding to your energy that is creating.

So for the first few weeks it does take reminding yourself and practicing changing your words that will change your energy from seeing any challenge as dead end. It will lift you up to see the detours so you can fly past them all.

Realizing Our Purpose in Challenges to Use our Psychic Abilities

Could it be that many of the challenges we are going through has such a silver lining of purpose that we may just need to be reminded of it. Maybe we planned these challenges so that we would remember when we birthed back into physical reality to overcome the challenges. Not in the old ways but in new sovereign ways, empowering ways as psychic or infinite abilities would allow us to do.

Some examples that I have used psychic abilities when in doubt and transformed the situation into a purposeful opportunity is if I have not heard from someone in awhile. I will remote view to check if everything is okay and many times through hind sight, after hearing from the person I found I was right on. If we there is something I want to resolve but the answer doesn't seem to come to me, then before going to sleep I affirm the suggestion to myself and also to remember my dreams and many times the answers comes through my dreams.

Of course the major one for most of us on this evolving journey and the reason you are reading this is because it's the path that has the greatest passion. If it is, then all the challenges have a great purpose of enfolding you to the urging and using your powerful abilities. It takes letting go of the old ways so that life can then become easier and simpler then the old ways. Like manifesting without big gaps in time and space, to be able to manifest instantaneously would surely make life so much simpler and easier. Or using telekinesis to turning a light off after getting so cozy in bed and then remembering you forgot to turn a light off. You could just think it off. I believe this is what our future will evolve into eventually the more the collective open up to psychic abilities as normal.

So when your are going through any challenges, think of them with this in mind and then allow your mind to expand into what your powerful purpose really is?

Your Purpose As Special Features on a Movie DVD

I love watching the special features on DVD's because they show us what is going on behind the scenes of the movie or whatever it is you are watching. Remember if you are watching you are involved because you are the observer affecting your reality just by watching.

If we used special features as our powerful purpose we can clearly see the similarity of the two. Using the analogy of the movie as our challenges and the special features as our powerful purpose we can then see the behind the scene's of what is going on. The only difference is when we watch a movie we watch the movie first and the special features last because we want to enjoy what is still unknown to us. In creating our reality the advantage of watching our special features first is that we can be the writers of our movie and create many possible end results. Then pick the one that has the most passion and excitement for us and go with that one.

Now we have our movie as our challenges, our special features as our powerful purpose and envision our purpose first. That way we then know our purpose for our challenges and then put all of our focus and energy into our powerful purpose. No more focusing on the challenge because the challenge was only there as a step to get to our purpose. Focusing on our purpose will keep us on track and keep us aligned with our desire already manifested. Your movie is done, you've put on the energy into it now you let go, trusting by knowing and expecting it will be done, it will be your experience in physical.

A present synchronicity that pertains to my website page

After writing this webpage I desired to find a video to add to it and the thought "Pleiades" popped into my mind. I remembered years ago that I read about the Pleiades teachings and resonated with it.

So I checked you tube and found this teaching. Barbara Marciniak and the Pleiades and what amazed me is that I picked and listened to part 8 which is the video I choose for you to check out if you have not seen this one. And part 8 said exactly what I intended to get across in this page about purpose in challenges. So it was not the other way around that I watched the video and then used it, I wrote the page and then found the video and it was the first one I picked out of over 18 part videos.

It showed me synchronicity and I am sharing my experience right now because synch occurs all of the time, but if we are not aware it will go unnoticed. Noticing is what empowers us to be able to perceive the connections of our thoughts and how it energizes to tune into a synchronistic connections.

Chapter 12

✳ ✳ ✳ ✳ ✳ ✳ ✳ ✳ ✳ ✳ ✳ ✳

INFINITE POSSIBILITIES

To open our minds to infinite possibilities we need to try to imagine that every thought ever thought still exist in the infinite hologram or infinite source of All That Is. It really is mind expanding when we ponder that in some great Source there is infinite thoughts that anyone or any being or thing has ever thought.

When we go beyond the physical plane of existence into infinite dimensions there is infinite possibilities of infinite consciousness and nothing is impossible. When we ponder into the realm that quantum physics has been showing us that there are infinite dimensions then we must expand our minds even further. Being stuck in linear perceptions really does limit our capacity to delve into the pondering of the infinite of All That Is. But when we do ponder into it we can then realize that the Infinite is expanding all of the time. So whenever any dimensional plane thinks thoughts our infinite source has already expanded more and it's on going.

The focus of this chapter is to expand our minds to more of the unlimited thoughts that we can choose to create more expanded experience for our manifested creations now. So we must expand our mind into the infinite possibilities to realize that many individuals on our planet are already doing and experiences some of these idea's that may seem impossible to the rational ego closed mind. However if we allow our self to expand we can then learn from these individuals who are doing things that seem impossible, yet are so possible because they are already doing it. They have accepted the new idea's of infinite possibilities and are experiencing them for themselves and it's become their wisdom. Their knowing that what seems impossible to the limited mind is possible to the open expanded mind.

On Vincent Daczynski's website you can read about his direct experiences with many who have mastered extraordinary abilities and he is also featured in the "What If the Movie" by James Sinclair."

Expanding into Infinite Possibilities is Evolving and Being on the Leading Edge of our Time

When we expand our consciousness we expand our beliefs and knowledge to know more for ourselves. Since we have always been creators creating our reality and the only difference now is that more and more of us are becoming to know it. This is empowering and expands us from old conditioning thinking of beliefs to expand into newer capabilities for our planet.

To be on the leading edge does take courage because many of our old beliefs really do have to break down into chaos so that the new structure can take over to support the new ideas of information. It's all part of evolving and we see it in technology and it all came from thought first. The creative, courageous minds that expanded themselves to bring technology to what it is today.

We are doing the same thing with reality as it continues to shift and expand into becoming more then what was believed in past history. We are shifting and evolving and eventually the mass of population will catch up.

So Where do we Find these Infinite Possibilities?

Let's start with the Psychic Phenomenon!
By psychic I mean using our focus to tap into the Infinite Consciousness and to get there we must become quiet in our thoughts and go through our Imagination. Our imagination is the door to the infinite where infinite possibilities are waiting for more to be discovered and where all great minds go! It's wisdom to realize that no one ever invents something to be more precise they are discovering it.

Many of our teachers or role models of the limited beliefs just didn't know, so how could they teach us and guide us into what we were naturally doing in the first place. It has only been a detour because now we do know and that is all that is important now.

Infinite Possibilities Expand into Infinite Capabilities?
Let's Take a Look At Some of Them

Let us take a look at the women Giri Bala has not eaten any food and has not consumed any liquids in over 50 years. It may sound crazy and impossible to the rational ego personality conformed mind yet reporters have traveled to see the women and confirm it to be true. She is actually quite popular as are many others that share their own experiences of not eating for years as can be seen on the "What If" movie and many other sources of information that can be further explored.

Here are other infinite possibilities that humans are capable of and doing.

• Individuals who are doing and experiencing telekinesis right now moving objects with their mind and intentions

• Healings of the most incurable diseases, spontaneous healing
• Growing in new sets of teeth
• Growing in new hair and natural color hair
• Improved eye sight to perfect vision
• Reversing the aging process and sustaining it
• Doing what psychic children and some adults are doing opening a rose to bloom in real time
• The man with x-ray eyes, others seeing through books, cards and walls, picking up energy through pictures and any objects or locations
• Levitation
• Remote Viewing
• Seeing auras
• Immortality

The list can go on and on because if you or anyone else can think of it then the thought already exists to practice to become masterful at whatever it is. That means that we have infinite abilities whether we are aware of it or not, we do. It just takes expanding your mind to accepting the infinite possibilities.

Chapter 13

✻ ✻ ✻ ✻ ✻ ✻ ✻ ✻ ✻ ✻ ✻

INFINITE ABILITIES

Infinite abilities are from the source of All That Is which is the infinite dimensions of reality. To access the infinite dimensions we must quiet our mind and focus on one thought. In doing that we are accessing our imagination that is the inner connection to the infinite dimensions of consciousness.

In spoon bending I focus on seeing and feeling the spoon already bent in my focused thought. I keep the focus until I feel the spoon become soft and warm in my fingers and then as I let go of the focused thought and I twist the long stem part of the spoon. The time will vary for each person's acceptance level of beliefs. It was the second day of focus practicing that I was able to twist my first spoon, for others it may be instantaneous, for some longer or never.

As I mentioned previously a great teacher I learned from was Nicole Whitney the creator and the host of "News for the Soul" her instructions made it easy to learn to bend spoons. It will depend on what we believe to be our truth of how long it will take or the possibility of it being experienced or not. Once we have already experienced it in our mind of focus, the physical experience of it will be dependant on our beliefs of what is possible and how long. Remember we are accessing through our imagination the non linear, anti gravity, non local of infinite dimension of consciousness.

Our linear physical reality is perceived in a slow down low vibration frequency that gives the illusion to appear that everything is separate. Our perception of reality is experienced as separate fragments of a past and a future that appears as an illusion that it's separate from our present. Yet it is in the present powerful momentum that we can experience and perceive everything going on simultaneously in infinite dimensions. It is by quieting the mind and being focused in the infinite manifesting dimensional source that will allow psychic infinite abilities to be experienced in physical reality. All it takes is practicing that we become better at it.

The Start of my Psychic Experiences

It is by sharing our experiences that others can also realize that the power is in all of us. Life can be as magical and powerful as we allow it to become by experiencing our psychic infinite abilities for our own selves. The more we do the more we evolve and grow with our feedback of proof that anything and everything is possible for us to experience in physical reality.

I started to notice my infinite abilities or psychic experiences when my grandmother passed away over 25 years ago. We were so close that she was like one of my best friends. My grandmother passed a couple weeks after my grandfather, her husband. The night before she passed we were talking on the phone and through our conversation my television that was on low instantly blasted in full volume. I would turn it down and then a few seconds later it would go loud again, this had happened over five times until I finally turned it off. Even after I had turned the television off it then turned back on again, so I unplugged it from the wall. I was talking to my grandmother the whole time it kept occurring and I became quite scared because I have never had that happen before. My grandmother asked me if I wanted to bring my two young sons and stay at her house over night, but since it was so late I decided not to.

The next morning I had received the news from my sister that our grandmother had passed away sometime through the night. My sister was the person who found her already passed away in her bed when she went to visit in the morning. When I got the news of my grandmothers passing I naturally had the intuition of the occurrence of the television the night before.

The message of intuition I interpreted in receiving was that it was my grandfather, my grandmother's husband was giving us a sign or communication of a premonition of my grandmother's death. It was as if he was trying to either warn us to do something or just let us know that he was in contact and knew what was going to unfold. Looking back in the next few days that followed I questioned myself that if I would have stayed over night would that have made a difference?

The conclusion of her death was that she was reaching for her heart pills but could not open the bottle to take them and suffered a heart attack.

My Knowledge turns to Wisdom through my Experiences

Looking back to the experience from my perspective now after 20 years of evolving and the wisdom of the nature of reality, I can see much more insights of the experience of that night of my grandmother's passing. I know now that any type of heart problems of our body has to do with the emotional blockages (as being stuck in an negative emotion) that we are experiencing that actually causes any illness or out of harmony of any disease of our bodies. And I believe that we do create our own death, though most individuals may not agree or be aware of that wisdom.

When we know we create every part of our reality it does mean that nothing is ever left out of that wisdom of knowing, then there is nothing we do not create. We can block ourselves from not being aware or in denial of some parts of our reality we choose not to understand how and why we would create certain experiences. We do create it all and that also equates creating our birth and death into other realities.

I do think that my grandmother was heart broken, so to speak, with my grandfather passing and no longer being with her physically. Even though it appeared that they hardly ever got along in their relationship, but I do think from all the years being together it was a major secure comfort zone for both of them. I think her fear of being alone and living without him subconsciously took its toll.

When we know that our body is always communicating to our self to take notice if we have any pain or discomfort. If we do not listen to the signaling it gives us it will become more intense, more painful until we do. It will try to get our attention to notice and correct the emotional stuff that is creating the stressed area of pain, illness or discomfort.

If we do not listen to the communicating signals then the pain or illness will progress even to die from it.

Back to the Past

The next day after my grandmother's passing as I was washing dishes and an ashtray that was sitting far from the edge of my counter for it to fall by itself, actually fell to the ground smashing into pieces. As I swept the pieces I actually said out loud, "Grandma I know this is you giving me signs and communication." My grandmother was a heavy smoker and using an ashtray to fall would be something I would instantly identify her with and the reason I know she used an ashtray to get my attention.

A few hours later while I was cleaning the bathroom I had a Nivia Cream jar that I had sitting again not anywhere near the edge of the counter moved and fell to the floor. Again I realized it was my grandmother again because she always used Nivea Cream for her face and continually told me that I should be using it too. Again out loud I spoke to her. At that time I had not even heard the word telekinesis or knew of any psychic knowledge. But I did believe in life after death because my grandmother talked about her beliefs of it.

I told others in my family about the experiences and that I knew that she was communicating with me to let me know she lives on in another reality and can communicate to me or any of us. I do not know how many believed what I was saying or not until the morning of her funeral at the burial. Just as the casket was being lowered into the ground we heard the loud sound of sirens traveling along the road it was quite the synchronicity. We all looked to the road and then to each other and after the burial we all talked about how that was another sign from my grandmother communicating to us. Then I realized that many in my family also believed what I was coming to know. My grandmother was letting us know that we live on and we are not just a physical body we are much more and death is just another adventure into another reality from infinite dimensions. And in many other infinite realities our psychic infinite abilities are already natural to us.

Beyond mere Illusions of Coincidence

After those experiences more and more experiences unfolded year after year as my life lead me to journeys that at the time I did not realize I would take. Whenever I look back in hindsight after I have expanded in my growth is when the realization would become to show me more of the nature of reality and more of my infinite abilities.

Every challenge became an opportunity for more evolving strength and growth and perpetually leads me to more wild and adventurous experiences. I am of course comparing myself to my own self because through half of my life I lived a reality of a pessimistic belief system and was lacking in self esteem and was sick most of the time. I lived in such fear and as a result, though I did not know at the time but however looking back now all the pieces fall into place. So for my own self I can now know the reason and the paths that I had to take to get me to where I am today. Is as different as night and day and then my psychic journey began unfolding now with a passion that sustained to continuing practicing to experience more of it.

Allowing myself to see through the Invisible to become Visible for me and that is what I believe all psychic infinite abilities and phenomenon is all about. It is not different, separate things in itself. It is a one unified field of our potential that we focus into and upon. Another sense just as our senses of touch, taste, smell, sight and hearing that we naturally use because that is what we birthed our part of our higher self into the physical form of our vehicle body. And it is the collective consciousness of this physical planet's accepted and natural use. When we expand to use more of our natural now seeming higher senses it is just another sense we are then tapping into or activating to use for our physical experiences.

For me it does not seem mysterious or paranormal and it probably does not for you either if you are still reading. Then we have come to know that any psychic infinite abilities we are naturally comfortable with using and evolving to use more. We then find it another part of our evolution of growth, making the unknown known. Eventually the collective consciousness of our planet will also grow into knowing and experiencing as part of the norm. Just as we adapt to new technology I believe will be the same with psychic abilities. It is our future collective being and is becoming more and more accepted each day as our planet continues to shift and change to allowing the new psychic infinite abilities to eventually become the norm.

For us to experience any psychic infinite abilities all we have to do is quiet the ego personality of the chattering rational and usually automatic thoughts which leads us from the finite consciousness to the infinite consciousness. To do that we use the process of meditation to access our imagination which is focusing our attention on one thought for an amount of time. Until the psychic infinite abilities become so natural and part of our everyday life. Depending on our soul or higher self purpose and blueprint theme that I believe we already set up before our birthing back into this physical existence again. And will be our guide of signs that keep us on our purposeful path if we keep our self aware.

Many individuals use their psychic infinite abilities right from birth as psychic children or from a very early age and became labeled as gifted individuals. However, we now know that everyone of us already has the gift, the abilities as a potential awaiting to activate and have it unfold into our life experiences.

Focusing is all it Takes to tap into any Psychic Abilities

Just as we use a camera and want to capture a clear focused close up of what we want to capture in a picture. The zooming in option allows the camera's lens to then remove any other background around what we will capture, so all we have to do is zoom in. Then presto we have our picture.

This analogy of the camera zooming in to see something closer, just as binoculars will give us the same affect is the same as focusing our thoughts. By quiet our usual chattering thoughts and instead focus our attention on one thing in our present moment for as long as we can.

Whether it is remote viewing, telekinesis, premonition, OOB, mental telepathy, premonition, OOB, instant materialization or transmutation, changing the past which behind that illusion we are really shifting realities. Whether it is teleportation, physical immortality, or any potential ability that we now label as impossible can be possible when we see past the illusions to know that anything is possible.

All and any psychic infinite abilities are not separate abilities they are all from the same infinite source, the quiet focused source of consciousness. When you can do and experience one of the psychic infinite abilities then you also can do and experience any other, they are all really one and the same. It is only our own belief that will block us to deny our abilities. Once we know it we then can open the flood gate to allow our self to become comfortable with all psychic infinite abilities. At first it may take awhile depending on your own level of acceptance in the timing of how long it will take for any psychic practicing until you experience it in physical.

Chapter 14

✶ ✶ ✶ ✶ ✶ ✶ ✶ ✶ ✶ ✶ ✶ ✶

QUANTUM LIVING

Quantum living is living our life with the knowledge that science, quantum mechanics proves through all the experiments what the ancient masters have always showed and taught throughout humanity is factually true. It is exciting because what was taught and believed of the old classical science and physics has to break down for the new model to eventually take over the new teachings. So that eventually everyone will incorporate it into their lives so that they are no longer the victim in everything but are instead a deliberate creator of their reality.

Just as many are now leading the way and many of us have already lived our lives this way before science proved it. I know for myself as probably for you too who are reading this, that you may have also learned the information from Channeler's and continue to do so. It was from our heartfelt intuitive knowing that guided us along before science had proved it.

Now it is available for everyone if they choose to know it too! Bringing to light the infinite possibilities, infinite realities, and the observer collapses the quantum state of the wave into a physical particle that creates the reality or the result from the observation that then becomes the experience.

We then come to realize that we have been doing it all the time it's the nature of reality as creators in creation. The only difference now is that in the past for the majority who did not know and believed that everything just randomly happens. That kept many believing that we were a victim instead of a deliberate creator.

To live the quantum life is to take all of our power back and live our life choosing our creations with the quantum knowledge that leads to our wisdom from our experiences. We have come to KNOW because when we have the experience for our own self, we just know. We're no longer stuck in beliefs because our knowing has taken precedence.

Living the empowering life in the most advanced way throughout our day, the quantum way. By having the knowledge and actually living it by being consciously aware of how we are creating each day that is creating our reality to be manifested.

Some Quantum Descriptions to Entangle Our Wisdom

For me I enjoyed knowing a little of the meaning of the quantum words and descriptions but leaving all the math and equations to the physicists. Many of us are similar and we just want the really good stuff that gave us more confirmation to whatever we were already doing.

Below I used Wikipedia's descriptions to define the meanings for some of the quantum language, for those of you who already know them then you may not want to go the rest of the ride on this page.

"Quantum mechanics

Wikipedia's description "Is a set of scientific principles describing the known behavior of energy and matter that predominate at the atomic and subatomic scales. The name derives from the observation that some physical quantities—such as the angular momentum of an electron—can be changed only by set amounts, or quanta, rather than being capable of varying by any amount. The wave–particle duality of electromagnetic radiation and matter at the atomic scale provides a unified view of the behavior of particles such as photons and electrons. Photons are the quanta of light, and have energy values proportional to their frequency via the Planck constant. An electron bound in an atomic orbital has quantized values of angular momentum. The unbound electron does not exhibit quantized energy levels, but is associated with a matter wave, as are all massive particles. The full significance of the Planck constant is expressed in physics through the dynamic physical attribute of action."

So in other words **quantum** is the describing the behavior of energy and matter at the smallest scales of our physical reality. Summarizing that a particle is a solid physical form and a wave is the subatomic properties of the particle's non solid form. It reminds me of our higher or whole self that is invisible but so real if we are in the allowing of our higher self or spirit or source, whatever you may label the larger part of yourself to come through.

Entanglement

Wikipedia's definition: "Quantum entanglement, also called the quantum non-local connection, is a property of a quantum mechanical state of a system of two or more objects in which the quantum states of the constituting objects are linked together so that one object can no longer be adequately described without full mention of its counterpart—even if the individual objects are spatially separated. " So it is two or more objects, minds link together even if separated.

As in telepathy you think of someone and they call or you pick up information about someone or something, regardless of the distance, then it is described as being entangled with them or it. When you affect external objects as telekinesis we are also entangled with the properties of the object. If you desire money you focus through visualization to entangle with vibrations of consciousness to manifest the desire fulfilled. Entanglement is connecting into the same vibration frequency, intertwined with another being, thing in its frequency range.

Superposition

Wikipedia's description: "Whenever two or more waves traveling through the same medium at the same time, the waves pass through each other without being disturbed."

So superposition is infinite states of possibilities at once, everything is a possibility until we collapse the wave then it becomes the reality the observer experiences, as in the observer effect.

Uncertainty Principle

Wikipedia's description: "In quantum physics, a particle is described by a wave packet, which gives rise to this phenomenon. Consider the measurement of the absolute position of a particle. It could be anywhere the particle's wave packet has non-zero amplitude, meaning the position is uncertain – it could be almost anywhere along the wave packet. To obtain an accurate reading of position, this wave packet must be 'compressed' as much as possible, meaning it must be made up of increasing numbers of sine waves added together. The momentum of the particle is proportional to the wavelength of one of these waves, but it could be any of them. So a more accurate position measurement–by adding together more waves–means the momentum measurement becomes less accurate (and vice versa)."

Coherence

Wikipedia's description: "In physics, coherence is a property of waves that enables stationary (i.e. temporally and spatially constant) interference. More generally, coherence describes all properties of the correlation between physical quantities of a wave. When interfering, two waves can add together to create a larger wave (constructive interference) or subtract from each other to create a smaller wave (destructive interference), depending on their relative phase. Two waves are said to be coherent if they have a constant relative phase. The degree of coherence is measured by the interference visibility, a measure of how perfectly the waves can cancel due to destructive interference."

In life we are doing it all the time as we are continuously choosing thoughts that are energy from the infinite waves of consciousness. Even if we are not aware that we are choosing the thoughts and leave it up to automatic thinking, at the deepest level it is still always a free will choice. So we can say that we have the powerful ability to choose from superposition states knowing we are the observer effect affecting our reality to be what we choose it to be. Meaning we are the creator's of our reality in every way.

To use an analogy of a tool being like thoughts that we use to direct our way through the waves of consciousness, of infinite channels of vibration frequencies to choose. Thoughts could be similar to a boat and our free will of choice or automatic choice is like the oars that get us around the ocean of consciousness.

Since I did not need quantum language in my life just the proof from the quantum experiments as sufficient enough to show me that I was living the quantum way. Quantum proof shows the evidence of psychic abilities and ESP and everything else that is contained in the extraordinary abilities and experiences ranges.

So in a nutshell and maybe for you too, we come to the conclusion that quantum mechanics is all about the awareness to know more about what Albert Einstein was quoted as saying, "Spooky action at a distance" which is learning more about the waves of the invisible part of the particle. The waves are the subatomic properties of a particle when it is collapsed into smallest properties of form, for myself in simpler terms it describes ... invisible.

The same as using the analogy of a coin, a coin is one objective thing that has and shows two different sides to it. It is like a physical being interacting with two different sides of reality, the physical visible (particle) part of our reality and the invisible to our five senses (wave) part of reality.

For science to finally become closer to what ancient masters have always known reality to be, this is the tipping of an eventual merging of religion and science however religion has too much dogma attached with it. So I think it is more appropriate to see it as science finally merging with spirituality. The powerful shift that is going on as our planet shifts and evolves.

Chapter 15

✶ ✶ ✶ ✶ ✶ ✶ ✶ ✶ ✶ ✶ ✶ ✶

PRACTICING THE PARANORMAL

Practicing of any paranormal or psychic abilities means that we must quiet the chattering ego thoughts. This practice has many defined labels that is popular and used as: meditation, yoga, focus, attention, concentration, unity of one mind, one thought, infinite mind and so on. I myself use the label FOCUS for describing any extraordinary ability to practice and become masterful at it. And so I will refer to FOCUS throughout this page on practices and experiences.

Focusing means to be able to think one thought for an extended period of time. At first you may find that your level of focus may only be for a few seconds. With more and more practice we actually rewire new connections in our brain and by practicing we become better and better at it. Until we are able to hold the focus for longer and longer periods of time, so from a few seconds of holding the focus on a thought to 5 minutes, to 10 minutes, 15 minutes and longer. It will always be dependent on your own acceptance level of what you believe is possible for you to successfully experience any paranormal ability. Then you let go by relaxing in the visualization.

Let go by knowing your are actually in a state of becoming, in a state of allowing your physical manifestation to experience of the paranormal or whatever information to just come through to you.

Imagination

Whenever you choose to practice the paranormal or anything else to manifest as the experience, what you are doing is suspending yourself into imagination, which is the non linear of infinite consciousness. However the length of time you spend in that pure focused state will be how profound the paranormal experience will be. As a result of you're practicing if you do it long enough it will become your actual experience of whatever paranormal ability you desired to experience.

The most powerful key is being able to focus and visualize or seeing yourself already performing or experiencing the paranormal psychic ability as already done in your mind of focus.

For example let's use the desire to heal or recreate our reality from the experience of a migraine. I realize I am categorizing self healing as paranormal because it is not accepted as a normal way to relieve any disharmony in our body. So it is still paranormal to the norm. First we must realize that we created the migraine from our own thinking that became our experience. Once we accept that as valid reality we become responsible for our creation and then we empower our self to change it. We focus on our migraine already gone, disappeared, visualizing by focusing on seeing our self go through our day without the migraine. Keeping the pure focus on that for as long as you can it will eventually with practice become similar to watching a video of yourself with sound and feelings. Whether you stay focused for a few minutes or ten minutes will be your feedback for your ranges of time spent in focusing until you just become to know it's done. Then you let go trusting and knowing it will become the exact experience in physical reality. We have created a reality of no pain and when we come out of our focus, we continue to hold our self as the being we desire. In other words if you still feel the migraine after your focus, continue to think of yourself without the migraine even if the pain is still there. If you continue to not fall prey to the pain, you will experience the migraine gone. I have done this numerous of times in the past.

Since I have transformed my thinking to empowering thoughts, I rarely create migraines in my experiences because I received the message loud and clear. It was always up to my own self to recreate what I created originally.

If it is data or information that you want to pick up as in remote viewing then you clear your mind in a relaxed state and focus on what you are intending to view or pick up information about. For example if you wanted to tap into information about a friend then visualize seeing your friend in your mind or thought of focus and just sit in a receivership state of being. If other thoughts pop into your mind just continue to bring your focus back to the one thought, your friends face or whatever pops in about your friend.

You do the same thing for distant healing, seeing whoever you want to extend healing to by focusing on the person and seeing them already healed.

Focusing does take practice and the more you practice it, the easier it will be to distinguish pure information versus ego chattering information. It is only through practice that you will become to know the difference.

Beginner's Practice

Many beginners start by using a lit candle to focus upon. By staring at the candle and keeping your focus of thought on the candle for as long as you can. Again whenever other thoughts pop up realize those other thoughts are trying to distract your from your purpose. Your purpose is to keep your focus on the lit candle flame and become one with the flame. As your practice to observe your length of focusing time and the ranges of how long you can extend it each time without ego thoughts surfacing.

I found it most important to be aware that whenever the desire you want manifested pops into your mind throughout your day, think of it in the way you want, instead of what you do not want. It makes all the difference in the energy you are adding to it instead of going back and forth and adding doubt. This also takes practice and I have found after a few days of practice it will become natural to trust and know its on its way to manifesting your desire.

I have experienced fire walking, spoon bending/twisting, breaking an arrow with my throat, breaking a board in half with one hand and remote viewing. Also out of body experiences, telekinesis, premonition dreams, telepathy, contact with other spirit entities and family members who have died, passed on all through **intention and focusing**. And of course I have experienced so many desires manifested throughout the years through conscious deliberate creating. I am working on the card practice of seeing through 52 cards too.

You can also focus and practice levitation and all other extraordinary paranormal abilities by focusing.

Have You Experienced the Other Powerful Benefit to Focusing?

What I have found for myself is that from years of practicing I can actually expand the focus of thoughts starting from when I awake and now focus on the thoughts I prefer and have them extend throughout the day. For me and if you have also found that you are able to do that too, it is a complete turn around from the ego based daily thinking all day long. The benefits are so amazing and powerful because it turns everything that was once negative into empowering thoughts. We all know the differences in negative thinking and empowering thinking by how it feels for us. The negative is all fear based thoughts and the empowering is love based thoughts. The ranges are so different in how it creates our feelings which then magnifies what we are creating all day long too.

The practicing of getting so proficient at doing this will seem uncomfortable at first and it does take commitment every single day and being self aware as much as possible all through each day.

If you are consistent at practicing it even for a month or two you will naturally continue because of the results of how you think, perceive and then feel about everything will change. You really do become empowered and blissful all day long.

We are in a Evolutionary Shift Taking Place

Now I have found that it may appear as there are two ways of practicing but really it is disguised as two ways but it is really one way. It is our own unique level of acceptance of what we believe we can experience through our practicing in the amount of time it takes us.

What I believe is going on is that as we practice any desired paranormal experiences or for that matter any desire we choose to experience we want to have, it will always vary depending our own belief system. So it appears as if we are practicing maybe for days, weeks, months even years on paranormal practices until we have the experience. But what I truly believe is going on is that we are constantly shifting realities, irrelevant of how long it takes, the shifting is still on going. Have your found this with yourself too?

This amazing information is from the greatest teachers that have shared the knowledge. It is then up to your own self to accept the knowledge and to incorporate it into your life. Then it will become an accepted comprehended belief transformed into knowing. As a result from entertaining the thoughts and then experimenting with the knowledge of information and from your own experiences will be when it becomes your wisdom.

We own it because we know it through our own experiences then nothing or no one can alter that wisdom of knowing for our self. Once we realize it as our truth then we know we are shifting to realities that contain the level of practicing and getting the results we believe are acceptable at each stage. No matter how it varies it is still the shifting of realities going on. It seems that we are teleporting beings without noticing that we are in fact always doing the shifting because of our linear perceptions. When we become to realize that we are infinite multidimensional beings it becomes to make more comprehendible sense and we resonate with it, then it is so amazing. For me and if it has for you then you already know that it's the greatest evolving process that we are creating for our present reality and future reality. If you have not realized or thought about it yet, then eventually you probably will, if you continue to expand in you're evolving comprehension to the new knowledge of information. Your experiences in life will become less normal and more paranormal.

It can be of the most important advantage for us to know this because it does change everything. When we can comprehend this knowledge of shifting realities perpetually then we can speed up the process of practicing time. Quantum jumping created and taught by Burt Goldman teaches how to quantum jump to connect with another self in the infinite dimensions that is already experienced in what we desire to do.

It Changes Everything

So now do you find that this information incorporated into our life can change everything? Instead of long practicing of any paranormal ability we can just connect or shift realities to the one we want to experience and wala it becomes the physical reality we experience. It still takes focusing, letting go and expanding our level of acceptance. Eventually we will be living our life the quantum living way, quantum living is using our paranormal abilities that creates our life to become magical and easier the way our higher self intended ourselves to evolve to become, paranormal into normal living in physical.

The possibilities are endless!

Infinite possibilities are then available for us to choose from once we become to absolutely know it for our own self. There would no longer be the need for the hard challenging ways to live and create our experiences in our life because everything would become bewitching, literally. That is what this new world shifting is all about, so that we can shift to the empowering ways to live and let go of the old worn out reality that keeps us believing we are the victims. We then become sovereign beings creating everything the way we desire to create and manifest, we become conscious infinite creator's.

Chapter 16

✳ ✳ ✳ ✳ ✳ ✳ ✳ ✳ ✳ ✳ ✳ ✳

SELF HEALING

"To Thine Own Self Be True"
William Shakespeare

Self healing is the most empowering way to not only know your own self but also evolve to trust your own self. It does take some practice for self healing if you are in a habit of trusting another to diagnose whatever disharmony that you have created within your body.

Our body will always reflect what is going on inside of our self first before we see the disharmony in our body.

Is Your Immune System Strong or Weak?

Our immune system is the collection of body cells that are either working together in harmony or working against each other creating disharmony.

What self healing really means is bringing the harmony of our body cells back into its natural flow. Since it's our own beliefs, thoughts and attitudes that created the body cells to become out of harmony then when we realize it's up to our self to choose to think better thoughts. The better thoughts will create better feelings.

Negative, hopeless, fear thoughts are low vibration energy and create panicky anxious feelings that we refer to as stress that creates our whole body to break down its immune system.

Our immune system will either be weak or strong depending on what thoughts we think that creates our beliefs we have come to value that create our attitudes about everything. If we are in fear, doubt most of our day then we will continue to sustain the creation of a weaker immune system that leaves us open to be susceptible to anything that comes our way.

I Have Been Self Healing Myself For Over Twenty Years

I think of my body as a mirror, feedback of my body's way to communicate to myself if it's out of harmony. Our body's natural process is for our body cells to work in harmony peacefully together, and it will until something affects the harmony. And what affects the harmony that blocks the natural flow is our thoughts beliefs and attitudes.

Did You Really Catch A Cold?

In self healing we do have to work backwards or opposite to what we have been conditioned into our belief system that everything just happens to us. The belief that we catch a cold, get a disease, or it just happens to us, came out of the blue is an illusion. The illusion or trick of our belief creates us to believe that we have no control or affect on our body. When we see through those illusions and limiting beliefs we then see the workings of how our thoughts and attitudes are creating our reality and our body's reactions. Our body is always communicating to us of what has been going on inside of it from our brain.

Let us take a look through the illusion of catching a cold or catching of anything that appears in the illusion of someone else or thing allowing us to catch something.

We were conditioned to believe that germs or viruses can be transmitted to us whether by touching something another sick person has touched or even through the air we breathe. What really happens is your belief which is a bunch of thoughts gathered together and you gave value to those thoughts, (usually unconsciously) that creates it to be a belief. This is what you then perceive to be happening under the illusion of catching anything.

In the example that you touch something that another person has already touched, let's say a telephone and now when you touch it your belief influences your perception that dictates that you just picked up some flu or cold like germs.

Then you start to notice yourself becoming warm or a running nose, coughing and whatever symptoms the other had that you may have just observed from them or from being told that other person who used the phone was sick with a flu or cold.

Your belief activates and your perception becomes in a defense threat mode (low vibration thought), you just touched the phone of the sick person's germs that are contaminated on it and now you are going to catch and become sick also.

Now I find this so interesting because that is what appears to happen, but it is not what is really going on. What is really going on is that when you touched the phone it was your beliefs that activated your electrical brain and body current from your thoughts to your body cells that you believe you can catch something that way. So it appears in the illusion that this is true. But what really went on was that your brain signaled from your beliefs of thoughts and your body actually activated the command as it is always doing to create the body cells to perform on command. The command was a threat, fear reaction that you are going to catch the same sickness as the sick person who touched the phone.

In reality it was the thought that activated the brain and body cells to create the sickness and not catching it from another's germs. This is something to give some thought to ponder if that is what you believe really occurs in that process because it shows us that nothing can be caught or transmitted to us through our sense of touch, or its in the air unless we **think** it can.

It Is a Trick Played Upon Us That We Miss

The trick of the illusion is of something being transmitted to us as catching something. We are never catching anything we are only tricked into believing that is the way it works. You may try to avoid such catching or transmitting of things, germs and viruses and so on by staying as far away from a sick person or disinfecting the objects before use.

Seeing beyond the trick of the illusion is so empowering because it brings you back to knowing how your brain and body does work. It also allows you to never be affected by any beliefs in catching anything. I can be around anyone who is sick in anyway and never be affected by the catchy tricky beliefs because I recreated new beliefs that give the new command. The command that tells my cells nothing can be affected as in catching something. And what a powerful way to live life because then you do not have to avoid anyone or thing if they are sick.

You then become sovereign in your health because you are the one choosing the thoughts that are creating the reality you are experiencing. Those new thoughts you choose become empowering beliefs that transform into your own knowing. And nothing or no one can ever alter that knowing for your own self because YOU JUST KNOW IT! You have experienced it for yourself.

Is Your Body In or Out of Harmony?

If we feel no pain or discomforts then our body is communicating and reflecting back to us that our thoughts, attitudes and reactions are in good shape, our natural process. We are instantly forgiving not doing much judging or blaming or reacting in negative attitude ways that actually only does harm our own self. When our body is feeling great we are already in the self healing harmonized sustained thoughts and attitudes. Then we know that our thoughts and attitudes are affecting our body and its reactions are healthy because we have kept our body cells in harmony and peace.

Trusting our self is being in a state of self healing by being aware of how our body is feeling is the absolute communication that keeps us in awareness and in health.

Whenever, there is any illness or discomfort that is the signaling for us to stop and ask our self some questions to self healing what is out of harmony. What thoughts have we been entertaining or thinking about lately on a consistent basis. Have we been using blame or self pity attitudes or become so stressed out over things, people, or situations in our life. How have we been reacting lately about all or some of these things? They will always be the clues that will mirror our feedback to what may seem mysterious when it appears that something has become out of alignment of harmony in your body.

If we are angry on a daily basis about things or others, or the world, regardless what it is, we must ask our own self, is it worth affecting our natural body's harmony of self healing because of it? When it comes right down to the most essential part of our attitudes of reactions, even if it is in our own thoughts not spoken to anyone else, our body is still picking up the messages, thoughts. If we do continue to then verbally discuss those angry attitudes with another or others we are really expanding more of the same kind of thing and our body is still picking up on it. There is no way of getting away from it.

If you have back pain ponder for awhile to find out what has been going on in your thoughts will be the beginning process of self healing. Have you allowed another to be a pain in your back to you? Because then you did give your power away to another to let them affect you, you didn't really have to. Or is there something going on in your life in regards to really important issues because that is feedback to show you that your back which is a very important part of your body. Your spine is the carrier of the rest of your body so important life issues can affect your back. Financial pressures can affect your back too since it is like a spine in your life. Or family members, whatever you believe is a strong (spinal) connection to important parts of you life.

What is also interesting to realize is that even if you hurt your back lifting something it still was connected to the previous thoughts about what you deemed important life matters to you. We must reverse if you want self healing to work by perceiving it this way. Did you have dominant thoughts about something, or someone that is important that has been bothering in you in your life then you hurt your back while lifting something, not the other way around. Hurting your back from doing something exertive was a reaction from the thoughts previously. Because if the previous thoughts were changed then you may have asked another to help you lift something and not hurt your back as you originally had. Self healing is bringing your body cells back into harmony thinking harmonious thoughts that create the harmonious attitudes.

Let's use another example of a sore throat and the desire you may have to self healing your throat. Ponder awhile about how you have been expressing things lately, negative or positive. What have you been thinking about that you have wanted to express to another but have not said anything maybe you could write out what you feel and then make peace with it and then throw it out. In a course I took years ago Dale Carnegie Leadership Course we were taught to hit pillows to get our any anger that was built up through the years and not released. What a releasing light feeling that is when you are done. The forgiveness comes so easily for yourself and to others who you believe hurt you in some way or whatever the releasing contained.

I did not need to do that practice very long because when I seen how my thoughts and attitudes was all connected to my brain, body and reality. I quickly became to know that it is dependant on my own beliefs, thoughts and attitudes in how my self healing would affect my body. And have been working that same process along.

As I have said before it may take some practice for you to do your own self healing if you have not done it before. If you have then you know how the self healing process goes. Either way it will always be seeing the connections between your thoughts and body to get to know what is really going on. And it is so worth it if you desire to know yourself and heal yourself and then be in the sustained health.

We could take every illness, discomfort, dis-ease and do the same thing with it by following it back to our thoughts and attitudes first, and then work it out from there, inner first and then outer. However that would take a book to link every body feedback to every possible thoughts we dominantly entertain and Louise Hay has done that.

Louise Hay's also teaches the importance of loving yourself first because when we love our self first our body cells keep that loving harmony. It flows outwardly in everything and everyone we encounter we then extend that love that transform our perceptions from our love thoughts and attitudes.

Practicing self healing will give you the proof and feedback for yourself from your body. Then you become to realize that it does not matter what another does or is that affects you, it is how you perceive it to be that will be what the affect will be to you. Will it be a love attitude or a fear attitude will make all the difference. You will know by as your body will always be the mirror and feedback to bring you back to your own self and work from there.

By making peace with everything, not only will your body reflect that feedback to show you by feeling great and healthy in its well being, you also will see your reality changing to the most amazing experiences. As I keep saying, your life will amaze you how blissful it will become especially when you do self healing while counting your blessings all because your brain and body cells received it all from you to begin with.

My Experiences of Healing

I have healed myself of flu's, colds, migraine's, sinus, reoccurring back pain that would also affect my legs, improved eyesight, depression, panic disorder, infections, sensitive gums, weight gain to weight release, my heart, body aches and much more.

I know this seems like quite a list of disharmony however they were all of my opportunities to experiment. The years of my journey to trust myself and rewiring my brain to be able to heal deliberately everything I had in my past creating without my awareness at the times. I didn't have the knowledge until I went looking for it and through it all I evolved into the wisdom of healing through my experiences for myself of how our thoughts, beliefs do create our body to be unwell or well. In other words in harmony of its natural functioning or in disharmony of it's natural functioning. I realized that I myself was getting in the way of my own harmony because of old conditioning programs.

I did it without a doctor or medication. My experiences proved over and over to me that we really are what we choose to think and that can become so empowering. It will always be from our own experiences to know the difference and the proof for our own self and if I can do it anyone can do it.

Chapter 17

✶ ✶ ✶ ✶ ✶ ✶ ✶ ✶ ✶ ✶ ✶ ✶

HOOPONOPONO

Hooponopono is really what this whole book is about, being 100% responsible for our self by being aware how we personally perceive others and everything and cleaning it up. It's how we create a sustained healthy body, peace when we choose to not alter our peace from reactions to old programs running in our subconscious. It's the knowing that "the world is in me" or in you and cleaning what we are perceiving what Dr. Hew Len says is our "data" memories. As Dr. Len also says, it's never about the other person or thing.

Why do we want to clean it up? To experience the sustained freedom and peace or bliss and instant manifestations with no effort as when we "clean data" in our own self we open a clearing or connection for the divine or infinite creator to come through. With all the attachments of data, old programs, subconscious memories or data to alter and distort the pure infinite and inspiration.

Hooponopono process is saying the words, "I am sorry, please forgive me, I love you and thank you" and doing it whenever data comes up which for most of us is constantly.

What I love about Hooponopono is that it's the simplest way, though not easy because we all have so much subconscious data going on all the time but it takes having to sort anything out and instead just do the statements over and over. It will surface deep data right on the spot and sometimes even bring you to tears as it did for me especially when it's data we have been stuck in for a very long time. It's when we say the words and then the feelings come with it from our heart and soul the release is so freeing.

If you really want to clear the connection for all the benefits of being a clear connection to allow the infinite divine, source come through then we do it all of the time, moment to moment.

Mastering Hooponopono Leads to Freedom

Anyone who has mastered total and sustained freedom in everything is being 100% responsible for everything in every way. They have mastered bringing everything to a neutral state of nothingness and created it to be the highest potential for their experiences. Its being a clear vibration or channel connected and open to Source or the Infinite Creator, the Divine.

Seth taught it as the "powerful present moment," Ramtha teaches it as releasing all of our past, Bashar teaches it by neutralizing everything, "nothing has built in meaning but the meaning we give it." Abraham teaches to clean our vibration, tune it. Jesus taught, "forgiveness" and in the book "the course in miracles" teaches also to give no meaning to anything and to see it in it's neutral state. So all masters teach it in their own unique ways and labels but it all means the same thing keeping the clear clean connection unaltered.

Old data or subconscious memories in not from the Infinite Divine it's old data playing as Ego v/s Infinite Being hell v/s heaven, good v/s bad, and it's all just judgments in our subconscious memories which Dr. Hew Len refers to as data v/s super-consciousness or infinite consciousness, it's all duality and separation from our Infinite Source or Divinity. Dr. Len Hew teaches how he cleans himself every moment with everyone and everything in his experience. What it's all about is Mirror Reflection work, keeping that invisible mirror on our self.

Hooponopono in Hawaiian definition "Hoo means cause and ponopono means perfection". Cleaning the data to a zero state.

So that every experience and every person and every object we come into contact with in every way. We pause and clean it up because it's always about how we are perceiving the data so that we can see it clearly without separation from our infinite source which is the Absolute Freedom.

Dr. Hew Len's Amazing Results

Dr. Hew Len "worked as the staff psychologist at a mental hospital for the criminally insane." "Patients were sedated and shackled. Employees quite on a regular basis. Yet they all were healed and released as Dr. Len worked on cleaning himself of what he calls data, our subconscious programming of recorded memories."

Now this is the most amazing proof of what Hooponopono can do, to have all the criminally insane patients healed and released without Dr. Len even seeing them.

My Beginning with Cleaning it Up

I started what I still refer to as the Mirror Reflection technique over 20 years ago from the Seth, Jane Roberts teaching. It does seem that though the labels have changed of it's teaching, it's the most profound work we can do. It sure does take moment to moment daily work on our own self so that we then reflect that reflection outward in the reality we are creating.

If you are having similar experiences from all the years of working on yourself but still have some big blocks that are preventing you from receiving your desires, this process will unblock them if you do them all the time and on everything. I released 5 lbs in a couple days without doing anything but saying the words.

As we clean the "data" for our clear connection with the Infinite Creator or Source. We're removing the data that keeps surfacing and being in an open clean state of being to see everyone and everything in their already perfect divine state. It's cleaning to allow the Divine Infinite Creator to experience reality in the way we were originally created without data or old programs of memories. Allowing the Infinite power of Infinite untainted love to come through us in physical

Total Freedom is Working through all that keeps us Separate from Infinite Source

All the masters teach **Joy in everything** and **being 100% responsible for everything.**

To be joyful and thankful with appreciation for the realization to know the difference is being thankful for the contrast or data so it can show us the opposite of it. Forgiving our self for not knowing and now being aware that will add to the releasing of the memories that have kept us separate from our infinite source. You will find that loving your own self will flow through experiencing everyone and everything else as loving.

It has made the most amazing difference in my life as I continue to do this cleaning or mirror reflection work all of the time The freedom is amazing when we come to know that we always have the choice in the moment to clear up our own data, or perception of what we see in others. For me it has totally changed my relationships with others and everything I interact with people, objects and situations and healing of any illness becomes natural.

Using everything and everyone as our opportunity to release the judgment memories that keep us separate from our infinite source, which is the Infinite Creator's Love Pure Power. Hooponopono allows us to clean by being aware by the moment and saying the words that cleans up the data that separates us from the infinite source.

Anyone or Anything You Experience is an Opportunity to Clean it Up

All other individuals that trigger our most lower vibrations as fear, doubt, anger can be our best teachers to reflect for our self using our inspiration of Infinite Power. It doesn't really matter who it is because if you have attracted them to you then it's your own reflection, your vibration that tuned them in and it's up to you to clean it up and Hooponopono is the most focused way to do it.

This is the whole point about making everything as joyful and fun as it can be. Removing all the judgments that dictate and create the illusion of working on ourselves to be tedious and drudgery, instead clean it up by perceiving it as fun and it will transform into a passion because you know it keeps you on a high vibration and an open pure channel from the Infinite Creator.

It actually can become fun when we don't take it all so seriously and just see it as another continuous opportunity to learn, expand towards our infinite source that then allows us to be free from the old memories that keeps us separate. Then you will be using Hooponopono to create your day your way.

Since you are reading this then just as my self and others who are on the leading edge of our sustained passion, our purpose this time round to know all we can about the nature of reality and how we can do everything we possibly can to clean it up with Hooponopono to live our life of our highest potentials. To become whole and eventually experience the freedom of sovereignty, and become our infinite divine self in physical by being a clean open channel that allows us total freedom.

Chapter 18

* * * * * * * * * * * *

PSYCHIC CHILDREN

Psychic children with these extraordinary abilities are popping up all over the world and have the most extraordinary abilities. There are many labels of names in defining these children including starseed children, children of the rainbow or children of the Blue Ray. They can perform abilities that will expand your mind to what was thought impossible to show that anything is possible.

These super children can read books, magazines that are picked at random with their eyes blindfolded and read through different parts of their body using their feet, hands, arms to read through. They are really picking up on the energy of whatever the object is holding.

The children are blindfolded and given pictures from the audience and can not only tell what is in the picture but give out information of the individuals in the picture. Of where they live, what they are going through or what they have gone through and other members of their family and friends.

Some of the psychic children influence opening live closed rosebuds. Audience members were holding roses in their own hands and the children just waved their hands and the thousands of rosebuds slowly opened into fully blossomed roses before the eyes of the amazed audience. It is under the strict discipline of scientific research, the Chinese government has observed these same children changing human DNA molecules in a petri dish. They remember their past lives and the purpose for coming here to help the world evolve. Just incredible!

Paul Dong and Thomas E. Raffill writes about the abilities that these children can do in their book, "China's Super Psychic's." Paul Dong teaches Qi Gong or Chi Gong which means "Energy Exercises" which is mental focus and breathing exercises.

It was also discovered that the children's DNA is not the same as normal human DNA. It seems that when we practice extraordinary abilities it changes our brain rewiring which in turn would change our DNA. The potentials for our empowerment are amazing when we expand our mind and brain to new unknown abilities like these psychic children as they are infinite creator's and are a role model for all of us. As in Norman Doidge, M.D. explains in his book "The Brain That Changes Itself" the plasticity of our brain. When we practice something we have not done before our brain rewires new connections.

Drunvalo Melchizedek interest and research in these children inspired him to bring this information of the children to the public with videos of the psychic children's abilities performed for audiences. To expand our minds as proof of how much more powerful we can become.

Chapter 19

✳ ✳ ✳ ✳ ✳ ✳ ✳ ✳ ✳ ✳ ✳ ✳

SYNCHRONICITY

Synchronicity was labeled or coined by Carl Jung from his experience with a patient of his. His patient had a dream the night before her appointment with Carl Jung of golden scarab and the next day during their psychotherapy session a golden scarab hit the window of the room they were in.

Synchronicity is Being in Alignment ... in Flow

Synchronicity ... I love the vibration of how it feels when I say the word because it has a powerful vibration kind of momentum tone to it. I feel it in my heart as an expanding feeling that has a powerful wisdom as a tool for us to use while we are evolving.

If we use the analogy of television and the signals through a satellite the satellite picks up the signals and transmits it through your own personal satellite unit that then directs all the signals to be the channels that you can watch. 100's of channels that you can choose are at the switch of your converter to choose whatever program you desire to watch. Even though world wide anyone with the same devises can also choose to watch any channels they choose also because it is available to all.

You choose by your own preferences. This is similar to consciousness with infinite thought vibration frequencies yet we choose the narrowing of channeling thoughts by what we are focused upon. Synchronicity is the aligning of the same frequency of similar thoughts that is like radar that tunes it in to match.

It is the same way for any reality we are experiencing from our generated thoughts of what we will be tuned into as a vibration that will be the frequency that we will experience as a reality, like a channel.

Now of course if you are not being aware then you may be having many synchronicities but are just not noticing them. It also has no judgments or conditions it will show us right on what we are thinking without any favoritism. So whether it is something negative or positive, synchronicity will show us either way. Again its all dependent on our own choice of thoughts to be using to experience the reality we are experiencing and also synchronized to.

When we allow our selves to become so consciously aware we will notice synchronicity through our every day experiences. And also notice the variations of the time gaps to when we thought about something and then the time gap of how long it took for the synchronized physical experience to match up.

Synchronicity can Give Us Great Feedback

Synchronicity shows us so precisely as a sign for our own feedback of what our ranges of whether we are right on or off by a bit or how off we are. If we are not noticing any synchronicity then that is showing us that what we think to what we experience in our outer physical environment is missing the frequency channel. This shows us we are out of synch by how far the gap may be if you become aware of it.

The feedback it shows us is how in tune our inner thoughts are with our outer physical experiences and how in alignment we are. It is a matching, the same as, being in tune, meaning no contrast or duality of opposition in the moment of the matching which is being in the same alignment of our thoughts. When we notice it and become more aware of it enough times then we will find more of it will show up for us. When we become to know what is going on when we experience being in synch then we appreciate it even more. As it shows us we are matching our inner thoughts that so quickly become our manifested outer physical experiences.

The variations of experiences can range from a small simple experience as words matching up with your environment. This frequently occurs when I would write with a radio in the background and just as I would write a word I would then hear the exact word on the radio. Either a word in a song or the announcer saying something using the exact word or phrase I wrote. Almost instantly I'd write a word and a second later I would hear it. There were times that this occurred on going for over an hour.

Another occurs quite often too, as we all experience a phone call from a friend you just thought about. Or desiring a hot coffee and a friend showing up without any notice and brings a coffee for you.

For a more predominant experience I will share with you another example. My desire for the home we had moved out of to sell as we already purchased and were living in our new home which was another vision we imagined that manifested. We wanted privacy, lots of land around us which was the complete opposite of the home we had moved out of.

Everyone was telling us how impossible it would be with the decline of the market and the home itself needing work and on and one with others opinions and judgments. But I held firm to my imagined vision of what was my desire manifested specifically. I had the absolute faith and knowing I could manifest it, all I had to do was imagine what I wanted and block out what anyone else was saying.

For a couple of weeks I did a focused visualization for just a few minutes a day of it already sold with excited feelings. Then I would just let it go and get on with my day and whenever the thought about the house came up I would think of my desired vision already manifested. I would not alter my vision and knowing for anyone or anything. Time was becoming desperately crucial too.

Then I received a vision of the exact appearance of a male and all the specifics. The next day we received a call from our agent telling us exactly what I had envisioned, exactly. Of the kind of male interested in our home and also a quick closing of the deal within two weeks. My vision was exactly right on with every specific I desired and manifested exactly the way I had envisioned it.

Now this has a mixture of many experiences in it. Not only to be aware of the gap of time from my first visualization and then the vision then the agent calling with the exact specifics of my vision and then the manifested deal closing. Though the gap of time was a couple weeks, it showed me the feedback of proof of synch and also my desire in specifics manifested.

So it appears to be that synchronicity is the outer manifestation of what our inner has already focused thoughts upon. The inner is what we tune into from infinite realities of consciousness and then through the alignment it manifests and shows us the outer physical manifestation. It is like a mirror for us to reflect from our synch experiences.

So being in synch just as any manifestation is possible, it is only limited by our own beliefs and our level of acceptance of what we expect we will create

My Journal

When I first became interested to learn more about synchronicity years ago, I kept a journal of as many synchronicity's that I could that I had during a day. Until it became a natural occurring experience that I could no longer keep track, there were so many experiences of it. What was most interesting for me was the variations of time gaps for some synchronicity's and yet on other days very little time gaps of what the reflection had shown back to me. It became a great tool to evolve as feedback for my alignment of inner to outer.

Synchronicity and our level of acceptance can also be great feedback in showing us what we accept in our own personal beliefs about everything and every area of our life. It will expand and change the more we evolve in being aware on a daily basis of the greatest mysteries as they become known to us.

CHAPTER 20

✳ ✳ ✳ ✳ ✳ ✳ ✳ ✳ ✳ ✳ ✳ ✳

CREATING YOUR OWN AFFIRMATIONS

For most of us we have used affirmations throughout our journey to remind our self as often as we can to stay or get back on the awakening path. Being and staying aware is the first step to changing what we no longer want to experience and then a new desire pops into our awareness of what we do want to experience. We can not change anything if we are not aware of what we are choosing to think that will be what we are focused upon that will be creating our reality we experience.

So affirmations are a great way to insert the new words or statements to our self when we notice that we are not speaking or thinking in alignment of what we desire to manifest. For an example lets say we have a sore throat, we are aware we have a sore throat and realize that we did create it so we can now recreate a healthy throat without soreness. You start by affirming to your self, your throat feels good, it is healthy and create more statements that support your throat being back in harmony and already healed.

By inserting the new potential words or statements it brings your focus of thoughts and feelings into healing stages instead of the other way around by focusing on the pain and ill health of your throat. Because you know that will only continue to create more pain in your throat.

Using affirmations like this for everything and any experiences you have in your life that you don't prefer and insert the new affirmation you do prefer until it becomes that experience for you.

Creating Affirmations for the Most Affective Creations

So we know that affirmations are words we choose from thoughts that are going to be potentially beneficial for our self. The most important part in creating new affirmations is keeping it in the present tense as I am healed, I am love and loving, I am wealthy and so on.

You may find in the beginning of saying affirmations that it may feel uncomfortable at first and the reason being is because you are still comfortable as a habit of feeling the reality you are presently experiencing. This is the reason you must stick to inserting the new affirmations into the thoughts you are going to choose and focus upon and then verbally express. The timing of how affective the affirmation will become will only depend on your own self and is different for each of us because its dependant on our own beliefs and levels of our own acceptance.

Just as everything else the more that you practice by doing it the more comfortable it will become to accept as you reality and how affirmations does work. The new empowering statements of affirmations will also trigger better emotions to feel automatically. So when there is anything at all you don't prefer to experience that's when you create and use the new affirmation.

A Few Examples of Affirmations to Use

I am Love, I was created from Infinite Love, the Source Creator of All That Is

I use every opportunity to evolve into my highest potential that overflows into everyone and everything I experience.

Everything is an experience, I learn and appreciate from the contrast of what I do not want to experience and now experience what I do prefer and want. I know the present moment does hold the power and use it to my highest benefits.

I keep my connection to the Infinite Source by choosing thoughts that are of high vibration. I love myself and that overflows to everyone and every experience. I am a creator creating my reality and accept 100% responsibility for it all and this keeps me empowered with the infinite source.

I am allowing and accepting of others, I know we are all on our own journey. I choose love and bliss and respond in the most aware conscious loving ways.

These are only a few examples and you can create from your heart what feels the best for your own self in creating your own affirmations. If you are new to affirmations you will find it so amazing how it can transform any negative or what you don't want to experience to be what you do become to experience, of your highest joy, love and desired manifestations too.

Chapter 21

✳ ✳ ✳ ✳ ✳ ✳ ✳ ✳ ✳ ✳ ✳ ✳

INFINITE WORDS MATTER

Using Infinite words will make all the difference. The words we speak matter literally. Words and our thoughts are energy that creates vibration frequencies that is creating our reality. We can observe how we speak in the words that we use and it is interesting to take notice that our **words are the end result of our thoughts and beliefs**.

Just as each letter as I am writing this page expands and transforms into words and then sentences and then a page full of information. When it expands further we then can accumulate a chapter and then a book is transformed into creation. This is a great analogy to show us how the thoughts we choose become transformed into beliefs which then become our words and our creation of our reality in an on going energy.

INFINITE MANIFESTING

Infinite words are different compared to the mundane normal words that we speak out of automatic limited beliefs. Limited words are words we use without any awareness of what we speak. So since words are the end result of what we think and creates our beliefs of what we think is true for us.

If our daily words are very limited, finite then that is also the vibration that will be the frequency of the reality we are creating and experiencing. If our words are unlimited, infinite then that will be the reality that we are creating and experiencing.

As we expand on our journey and choose to use infinite words we evolve from finite to the infinite and are constantly changing. Our beliefs are also changing from choosing infinite words from infinite thoughts that are being created as we evolve and our consciousness expands. Which may even leads us to go beyond into more unknown ideas into experiences that we can evolve even more, making more unknown known.

You probably have already noticed many of your words that you now use also have changed to support the evolving you. Words that in your past self you may not have noticed or used are now a part of your everyday words.

There may be another evolving thing you can do that will also allow your expanding infinite expression to evolve which is creating new words from the infinite source. Because as you evolve everything does change about you and your reality, so when you allow infinite words to be expressed through yourself you will find that these infinite words are a unfolding of the infinite you that is expanding.

Infinite Words from the Creative Infinite You

When you use infinite words the creative you starts to flow. It is when you have new experiences and creativity flows that these new experiences are from the infinite source which means the words become unlimited also in your infinite expression.

Words are the end result of what we become to express in our talking and communication to others, so if our words are from the limited consciousness then they will always show us what our beliefs are consistent of. As we evolve we are experiencing new experiences and the new words when we allow ourselves to create as a result will be infinite words. And anything from the infinite consciousness will seem new to the norm limited consciousness of reality.

When we experience feelings of passion, serenity, bliss, ecstasy, elation, nonjudgmental love, infinite unconditional love these are feelings as a result from thinking infinite thoughts. These expressions are the evolving YOU having the experiences of the infinite life that is becoming more natural on a daily basis.

When we experience feelings of depression, hopeless, of fear, doubt, anxiety these are a result from thinking finite thoughts. These expressions are not evolving thoughts they are automatic thoughts from old stored memories.

Moving Beyond the Ordinary to the Extraordinary

Have you ever experienced creating new words for your new experiences? It is quite the amazing experience when we allow what we are experiencing to flow into our expression into words.

For an example when I am having an infinite experience of elated joyous bliss and feeling ecstatic then I find that words come out of my mouth that would make no sense if someone was listening with a limited perception. Because that individual would just think I was out of the ordinary or crazy because they still do not have a comprehension, or belief system to support beyond the ordinary infinite experiences.

When we do something out of the ordinary we are evolving from limited consciousness of the ordinary. So we are going to be doing and expressing in the most extraordinary ways.

Infinite Expressionary

I have created my own dictionary of infinite words that I have allowed to verbally flow that describe meaning as an outer flow of expression of my experiences. I have written in the definition of the new words of what they mean for my experience to express it beside each word I have created.

"INFINITE IDEAS CREATE INFINITE GENIUSES," my quote, since we are being creative we must allow the creativity to flow and honor our creations. As we all are potential genius's, just as we all have ALL POTENIAL in all of our abilities when we allow them to become activated or to expand in our evolving nature.

If you have never tried this, you may also experience the expanding fun in it. I created a **Infinite Expressionary** that really does come in handy. Any time that I have allowed myself to become into a downer mood, or negative reaction I read my **infinite expressionary** and read a couple words.

What this does is trigger the memory of the experiences I had when I created the infinite words and then as I continue to read more words and the definitions, my spirit become aroused and next thing I realize I am flying high again in creativity and bliss.

Infinite Expression Fun Experiment

Do you remember the Walt Disney movie **Mary Poppins** and the word in the movie that became quite famous, **supercalifragilisticexpialidocious**?

It took a very genius creative mind to not only create the word but also Disney World and all the great movies. Walt Disney was definitely out of the ordinary, wouldn't you agree?"

Now if you allow yourself to be ready then let us give it a try right now, remember you are now going into infinite creativity.

Do you have a paper and pen handy? Great then allow yourself to relax and think of something that would be the most fantastic experience for you that you would love to experience in your future. Let it be something that is so exciting, so elated, so fabulously amazing!

Just think about by imagining it for a few minutes and really get into the feeling of living it as if it was really occurring in your reality. This means quieting your mind to only being presently focused on doing this imagining until an infinite creative new word comes through your mouth and you then say it verbally and write it down. Then write a description of what it meant for you beside the infinite word.

Of course this is what we do when we are creating our future, meditating, remote viewing or any other psychic practicing. It is the same process of going into our IMAGINATION, the infinite mind, or infinite source, or quantum field, different words to describe the same thing. And the way to get there is to quiet the chattering mind to focus on one thing.

So are you expressing by saying the word that flowed?

My word that flowed out is, "**surrealtomuntious**" that is what I was feeling. Since I was focused on creative creating there was no other finite normal conventional word that really could describe my feeling from the experience I was having, which allowed the flow of a word that I created to now describe it.

Synchcanotious...

Have you wrote it down and described it? Great!

As you add to it and use your **Infinite Expressionary** you will find incredibly amazing creative flow continue in your daily life. You will amaze yourself and experience the genie of your genius in infinite ways.

Chapter 22

✳ ✳ ✳ ✳ ✳ ✳ ✳ ✳ ✳ ✳ ✳ ✳

HIDDEN MEANINGS IN WORDS

Many of the words we use have hidden meanings that probably go unnoticed because we use them so automatically. We use words everyday to communicate to others when we verbally speak. I found it fun and interesting in revealing some words that simply do reveal hidden definitions to their true meanings.

These are only a few words however the hidden meanings is placed in the words when deciphered. I think it's fascinating and probably whoever originally created certain words did it with the meanings intertwined in the words. Just like reading between the lines when we read and seeing the exuberant meaning in movies too

Hidden Meanings in Words

Belief ... inside the word there is a root word **LIE**, I find that amazing as it shows us the hidden meanings of what belief really defines. In a positive perception we can realize it as beliefs are fluid, flexible and changeable ... when we create new experiences that become true for ourselves, then an old belief changes to a new one that supports our new experience.

Belief ... If we add a 'D' in front of the letter 'ie' and remove the 'bel&f' in the word belief the word becomes '**DIE**' ...which can gives us a definition of die, or put to death, to put an END to all false beliefs, old limiting thoughts, ideas that hinder our empowerment, our Creator Esteem. Transformation to real truth, no more lies, the death of ignorance into the rebirth of knowledge transformed to wisdom through our own experiences. Because be**lie**f is a lie and changes, the **die** part is the death, end of the many old beliefs that no longer support our new experiences that we KNOW to be true for us.

Christmas ... has **Christ** and **Mass** in the word, Christ who is a symbol of our brethren, sibling, same DNA as us. As in Jesus is God's son, which makes us sons and daughters of God or the Creator too! Christ in mass population may mean that we activate the same Christ/god DNA in our bodies as Christ did, then eventually it will become in mass reality through evolving when it becomes a mass valued belief into knowing. That we are also are inherited with God and Christ DNA heritage in our own selves.

Coincident ... **coin** is the word in the beginning of the word coincident, meaning it is one object which has two sides to it ... negative/positive ... and also has the word 'I' coinci"I"dent in the centre of the word, hidden meanings of I, our own self has two parts of a whole, the altered ego personality and our higher self, the 2 merged together allows us to become powerful evolved knowing beings.

Compassion ... remove the last 3 letters of the word then it reads **compass** which means to use as a direction...compassion may be the energy of direction we need to use everyday to transform any negative to a positive. The last 3 letters by removing the first 7 letters read **'ion'** which is the is an "atom or molecule in which the total number of electrons is not equal to the total number of protons, giving it a net positive or negative electrical charge".

Disease ... die, in the hidden word in the beginning of the whole word is **DIE**, yes a disease can create death. It is disconnecting from the ease of harmony that the body cells naturally function, how it was created to function in **ease** that is also in the word disease when we remove the 'dis' to spell 'ease' ...'dis-ease' and flow naturally of higher vibration thoughts and feelings. When it functions in opposite of EASE, then the harmonious ease flow is blocked, tension results and closes the natural flow to become blocked and stressed upon thus created the dis-ease-ment.

DNA ... spelt backwards spells **AND** ....which means to extend, add to ...

Earth... when we take the last letter of the word "h" and move it to the beginning of the word it spells **Heart**. Showing us the hidden meaning to reveal that we are connected through our hearts to our earth in amazing ways.

Ego...e-go ... can be looked at if 'e' and the 'go' symbolized energy, then energy that can guide us away like to eGO, 'e-go' from our higher self, but if we transform our eGO to merge itself with our higher self or spirit, transforms, merging with god, love of what our true potential is to become.

Emotion ... by removing the "e' in the beginning letter of the word it becomes ...'e-motion ... the word **motion** is in the word emotions shows us that motion is a moving energy ... 'E' can symbolize energy, energy in motion, and is exactly what our thoughts are made of, energy. Emotions are scattered throughout our body, when we funnel it through focus, the scattered emotions become genuinely heart felt feelings, the most powerful in creating reality. We must also be aware that we are addicted to our emotions and that can prevent us from creating the reality we prefer.

Evil ... spelt backward is **live**, and if we add a "d" in front of the word it becomes devil, may mean, to live by the de-evil-ish ego personality that can be destructive, create dis-ease in the body and the planet by separation and judgment of life from love that heals and is a powerful vibration.

Evolve ... rearrange some of the letters to spell ... **love** ... the way to evolve into god-like beings is to love, and to activate the god gene in our DNA.

Fantasy ... spells **santa** from the word 'fantasy' when we rearrange the letters, which symbolizes gifts, giving, being of service, happiness, joy, excitement, sharing...
Fan-tasy also has the word 'fan' in it to symbolize movement, we could find the hidden meaning to be in movement of a santa, christmassy spirit in our daily life. And the word fantastic to just add a few letters to the word and remove the 'y' of fantasy, which reality is becoming to be more **fantastic** from fiction to non fiction.

God ... add another 'O' to God to become **good**, GOoD ... the best feelings that can extend to all...

Good-bye ... the hidden meaning could be saying good-bye to the hellish way of greeting anything or anyone '**hell**-o ... first four letters can show how things can be HELLish when we greet individuals or life with a negative, judgmental ego perception.

Health ... when we remove the first letter 'H' and replace it with the letter 'W' it spells **'Wealth'**. Being healthy and or wealthy is all dependent on what we believe, everything is energy and dependent on what we choose to put our attention and focused energy upon that creates us to be in the state we will be in.

Heaven ... the word **heave** by removing the letter 'n' at the end of the word, heave-n, is to push or pull together, just as what we are doing in creating the new world of heaven on earth ... and both heaven and earth have 'EA' in the words. If we add the 'H' from heaven to earth we get H-earth ... we get a hidden meaning of fire, warmth, a fuel ingredient when we are creating, the fueling of the feelings in the heart-h ... when we take the word 'hearth' and remove the 'h' from it we get **heart**.

Jesus ... the last two letters can show **US**, meanings of unite, unity all parts of one, parts of US, and that we are like 'Jes-us', we have the abilities and empowerment within us to even do more than he did.

Know... is a very powerful word with **5** hidden meanings of words from the one word.
Know remove the 'K' letter in the beginning of the word know and we get **NOW**
Reverse the letters in 'NOW' backwards to spell and become **'WON'**
Rearrange the letters in 'WON' to become **'OWN'**
Then remove the letter 'W' in W-on to become **'ON'**
Know, now, won, own, on. To **know** that the power of creation is in the powerful present **now**, we become to **own** the knowledge and we **won** by being right **on**.

The hidden meanings of how to K-now is to create consciously with awareness and powerful energy as it is knowing and creating in the powerful NOW, the present. To 'KNOW' is to be in the powerful state of 'NOW', and knowing that is empowerment. To know is to never mislead ourselves because it comes from a heart felt feeling that we just know to be our own truth. Once we experience something that was unknown to us previous to it being unknown, we then just know it, we own it.

Law ...spelt backwards and removing the end letter 'L' becomes **WAL**, we know that a 'wal'l is a thing to divide, separate. Laws are always changing and laws are motivated to control, which limits any type or freedom or sovereignty. Removing the letter 'W' from the beginning of the word for it to become **AL** 'al' to add another 'L' would become for **ALL**, which law does intend all to follow.

Life...the **if** ... 2 letters in the middle of the word life can show us that 'if' is filled with possibilities. And can be a hidden meanings perception for quantum physics, of everything in life being a probability, possibility, which it is until though our focus of attention, whether aware of doing it or not (it is the mechanics of creating) bringing all possibilities into solidity of physical form. The particle/wave duality.

Menopause ... by removing the 'meno' in the beginning of the word then spells to become **pause**, to pause, contemplate in life to merge the female & male, ying & yang, into emergence of two polarities into ONE.

Now ... spelt backwards Won, meaning to truly really win in anything, is to be in the powerful NOW. When one stays in the powerful present state of NOW, it is a winning of the greatest power. What we think and how we think in the present of NOW alters our past and is also creating our future. Simple as that!

Peace ...spelling the word peace as it sounds changes the 'c' to a 's' sound, P-ease, shows the hidden meaning of **ease**, which is to be in harmony, in ease, easy flow with the flow of ease.

Rebel ... has the spelling of 'bel' at the end of the word and bell has an attachment for many of a ringing, which is a pleasurable sound. To rebel against a man made law in Gods world would be a positive God like quality of no conditions or judgments.

Secret ... rearrange some letters to become **secrete**, allow to flow outwardly, would also be to dissolve the secret to SHARE with others, secret could mean to be kept in greediness the opposite of sharing and trusting,

Self ... remove the 's' in the word S-elf to spell **elf**, the hidden meaning of what we are, magical, powerful in our own selves when we expand ourselves to experiences to know it. To add the 'S' back into the beginning of the word shows us S-elf our powerful self.

Similar ...put a "I" into the end of the word, it becomes LIAR , in meaning, things may appear to be in likeness, sameness, when in truth there is so much uniqueness webbed throughout. When we unite the similarity we can then unite, which transforms the lie to truth by shifting our perception of it.

Your ... removing the 'Y' spells **our**, our is a unified meaning, and your is meaning another ... a hidden meanings of connections.

PART TWO

PSYCHIC EXPERIENCES

Allowing the evolving self to flow into the amazing empowering psychic journey of experiences that leads us into a life of ease, flow and love.

ANNAMARIE ANTOSKI

Chapter 1

✱ ✱ ✱ ✱ ✱ ✱ ✱ ✱ ✱ ✱ ✱ ✱

OUT OF BODY

OOB is our natural experience when we allow the knowledge to transform into our own wisdom from our own experiences to realize that we are really spiritual beings having a physical experience.

We came from a spiritual dimension birthing into our physical body. Our body is the vehicle that our spiritual self uses while we are in the physical plane of existence. Since our whole spiritual self cannot be wholly contained in our physical body, the part that stays invisible is our higher self that guides us on our purposeful physical journey. Our ego personality seems to lead the way until we connect again through awareness and knowledge or remembering our higher self.

We can use the analogy of the use of our physical vehicles that transport our body around from location to location in traveling. When you purchase another vehicle to take the place of the older vehicle, can be the same type of idea as our spirit in our body to transport us around the physical plane. If our body breaks down in disease and we subconsciously choose to end this trip for now and we use death to do it. Our spiritual whole self is then out of its physical body vehicle for our next adventure of experience.

Where Our Mind Wanders Our OOB or Spiritual Self Is

Try it right now. Sit quietly and contemplate any thoughts at all, remembering some past experience from your memory, you are actually recreating the past. Or think of a future experience you desire to have, the spirit part of you is actually in that future dimension. Or as you look out the window watching the birds flying that is where you are for the moment. It does not matter what your focus is upon with your thoughts it will always be where you are.

Do you see what I mean? No matter what it is we cannot escape the POWER OF NOW and our spirit part of us. Everything else is just a memory or choosing other dimensional realities of thoughts but we are always doing it in the now and it will be where we really are.

If we are thinking about another person in pure unaltered thoughts, we are OOB. It is a trick of beliefs, a trick of our senses to believe when we are in pure focused thought that we are always in our body. But if we ponder awhile we have already drifted into the powerful dimension of imagination. We have left our body for the moments that we are so focused on another or whatever focus we are putting our attention on. Behind the illusion, or belief trick, we are really OOB and visiting with another while our body sits in our chair taking care of itself as our body was designed to do.

The Sensation of OOB

We have all had the experience just as we are about to fall asleep or sitting in a serene surrendering relaxed state and felt the sensation of our body feeling really heavy. Then something inside us wants to release. We can feel our self becoming huge as a sensation and everything we perceive becomes huge in magnification as we float with the sensational feeling. I have had these experiences many times before I knew what was really going on years ago and would become fearful as the feeling was so unknown. I would stop it by closing and open mind my eyes quickly a few times to stop it from progressing further.

That is an aware starting of OOB experiences. When we go with it long enough and let go of the fears so that we can be comfortable with the OOB sensations as it starts to lift us upward away from our heavy condensed physical body, we can then progress. We will find our self actually traveling in a floating sensation through our house, out the door, outside and encircling the outside perimeters.

When we become really comfortable with the experiences after some practice then we can travel OOB to anywhere we desire. Another country, above the clouds, above the planet, other planets, anywhere we desire to go. Just as every out of the norm experience will take having the experience to know it for your own self and the validity of your experience.

I had my first conscious OOB experience at a fire walk seminar I attended years ago. All of us in the seminar were lying down so relaxed listening to a recording that brought us into a deep meditative state. I felt my body become so heavy while simultaneously I felt another bigger yet light part of me lift. This other part of me that I now refer to as my higher self seemed more aware, more intense and connected with the clearest perception ever. With such clear vision that can even be described, I could see the room with my body and all the bodies in the seminar lying on the floor.

I lifted even higher through the ceiling and then higher while observing all of the landscape with streets. Then higher and viewing the city to becoming as small dots as I swept along to view in even higher dimensions. Above the clouds and so challenging to describe but it felt like I was one with the universe yet uniquely aware of my separate part too. It seemed to last for hours then next thing I realized I snapped back into my body feeling so heavy and bliss started to fade back into the sensations of my physical body.

We are OOB when We Dream

Another experience we all have just as we are falling off to sleep and then you feel that floating and or the JOLT, like a big SNAPPING movement that jolts you back into awareness or wakes you just as you start to doze off. It's an awareness of what it going on every single time you fall asleep. Most times we will not notice it if we have our thoughts so preoccupied with what we are concerned or visualizing before we fall asleep. But if we consciously be still and focus on OOB we can be aware of what is going on.

In our dreams we are out of body and traveling and experiencing infinite dimensions that most individuals shut off from their normal daily experiences. All it takes is focusing and desiring the experience with enough passion to allow yourself conscious access to what you are doing so much of the time already but without your tuned in awareness.

For more information on OOB wisdom Monroe Institute is a most exuberant site of information. You can also listen for free to an audio program on News for the Soul, MY BIG TOE with Tom Campbell.

More OOB information on Tom Campbell's website filled with his experiences and his seminars.

My Second OOB Experience

My first OOB experience was at a fire walking seminar and was so amazing and serene and lasted a long time. But my second OOB psychic experiences I had many years ago also stands out in my memory because of the scare I had with it.

I had been writing at my computer for awhile and it was getting late and I was tired. I sat at my computer in a meditative trance just staring at the window and it was dark outside and I just sat there staring. Next thing I realized I was out of my body and looking down at myself on the computer staring out the window. It was such an amazing experience because just as my first experience years before that one I felt such a peace and empowerment with wisdom. No fear or doubt just peaceful bliss and freedom.

After a few minutes my son came into the room, he knew I was on the computer because many times the sound of my fingers typing for hours on the computer would wake him. But this time he came in and looked at the computer and then started screaming, "Mom, Mom where are you?" Repeating it many times and behaving as if he could not see me at the computer. Meanwhile I was still OOB watching it all. Then within a few more minutes I popped back into my body and was screaming back to him, "I am here! Cant' you see me right here on chair?" He kept calling for me even after I was back in my body and now it started to scare me because I thought I was dead, passed on. Then he started to laugh and that finally broke all the emotional drama and tension that was going on.

At the time he was studying acting and had been an extra in a couple movies, however when all the drama went on that was the last thing for me to think of that he was joking around and practicing his acting.

It was awhile before I had another OOB experience because of the triggered memory of fear of not coming back into my body, however once you experience it enough times, just like anything else, it becomes a natural experience you enjoy doing. Then even the fear of death dissolves and it propelled me to more psychic experiences.

Chapter 2

✱ ✱ ✱ ✱ ✱ ✱ ✱ ✱ ✱ ✱ ✱ ✱

TELEPATHY

Telepathy is going on infinitely and is what we use to create reality because we are always picking up on thoughts from consciousness. It is estimated that we pick up on over 70 thousand thoughts a day. And I do not think we could ever be reminded enough that what we think about most of the time is what is creating our reality.

Let's not Allow Names to Confuse Everything, Remember the famous statement, "Keep It Simple"

All words are the naming of everything to describe a meaning and created from others in our past and it's what we use every day for our language of communication. So someone created the words that we all use as a definition to describe a meaning to the words and many words have been altered or changed through history.

Words are the end result of our thoughts, so when we are referring to the word telepathy it really could be merged into realizing that all thoughts are from consciousness that we are picking up from with different levels

So then if we perceive all psychic abilities as another sense and just wrap it all up into a sixth sense. Instead of naming each ability to give definitions that they are all different from each other when they all come from the same Source. That Source is consciousness where every single thought from every being is infinitely recorded, so to speak.

It all Start's with Thoughts ... What is a Thought?

This is the description from Wikipedia, "Thought and thinking are mental forms and processes, respectively ("thought" is both). Thinking allows beings to model the world and to represent it according to their objectives, plans, ends and desires. Words referring to similar concepts and processes include cognition, sentience, consciousness, ideas, and imagination."

Wow! Now talk about keeping it simple and yet powerful in just a few sentences. Notice how many creating words about reality is webbed in the above description. Firstly "thoughts are mental forms", so they are inner, subjective. "Thinking allows beings", they did not even mention what kind of beings, which implies not just human beings but all beings. Animals, aliens, humans, all beings I suppose would be using thoughts. And "we use thoughts to model our world according to our objective, outer plans, ends and desires." So we do know that our inner subjective mental thoughts creates the outer objective desires, not the other way around.

So it all starts with thoughts and we can chose from infinite dimensions of thoughts and it is all dependent on what frequency or levels of consciousness we are choosing from. Whether it's from social consciousness of thoughts or higher vibrations of thoughts the variety is endless. Its similar to all the different choices of channels for viewing on television or radio's, except infinite dimensions have endless choices of thoughts.

Thoughts are what makes up consciousness, the Mind Of God, or the Mind of the Creator, the Source, Universe, whatever label you use, it's all referring to the same thing.

Telepathy

Let us take a look at what Wikipedia's description, "Telepathy (from the Greek, tele meaning "distant" and pathe meaning "affliction"), is the ostensible transfer of information on thoughts or feelings between individuals by means other than the five senses (See Psi). The term was coined in 1882 by the classical scholar Fredric W. H. Myers, a founder of the Society for Psychical Research, specifically to replace the earlier expression thought-transference. A person who is able to make use of telepathy is said to be able to read the thoughts and stored information in the brain of others. Telepathy, along with psychokinesis, forms the main branches of parapsychological research, and many studies seeking to detect, understand, and utilize telepathy have been done within the field."

So the term **telepathy** was coined in 1882 by the scholar Fredric W. H. Myers, a founder of the Society for Psychical Research, specifically to replace the earlier expression **thought-transference**. Thought transference is really being in the same thought frequency and telepathy then are the same thing because Fredric Myers created a new name to label thought transference to telepathy. **Mental** means inner, subjective, not experienced with our five senses. Since telepathy is thoughts then mental is **Extra Sensory Perception** is a named label to define not using our five senses but using an extra sense for any ESP experiences, including telepathy, which we could label our sixth sense. Without thoughts we would not be able to create reality.

So to describe it simply is that telepathy is picking up **thoughts** by being in the same frequency of another's thoughts. Either from others without using any devices or verbal communication other then our thoughts that creates our feelings. The most popular experience is thinking of a friend and within minutes your friend calls you.

Being Aware to Notice

This happens all the time with my mother, almost every time I call her which can vary as there is no consistency to my calling her, I just get the feeling that is generated from her thought to call her and do. Then she tells me "I was just thinking of you and then the phone rings and it's you."

There are so many experiences that can go unnoticed if we are not aware when they occur, however we are picking up on thoughts all the time. It will be dependent on what we are choosing to **tune into** of what we will receive. Also the more that we recognize the experiences the more we will notice more of it occurring.

We have all heard many stories and you may recall your own experiences of a KNOWING that you received as a vision or thought of a loved one and then later received a confirmation of exactly what you envisioned or thought did occur. Or of even unrelated incidents that you later may hear on the news and knew it before.

So we can realize that ESP is all intermixed and connected because premonition is in the mix too. If we are picking up data of information then it can also be a premonition, future thought reality or dimension that has not occurred yet in our physical reality. Our reality is slowed down into more solidified reality of time being perceived in slow motion as past, present and future, linear time in space. However in the higher dimension where all time is occurring simultaneously it is available to pick up on thoughts, telepathy and our physical time of picking up the information then seems as premonition. Still all the same thing really, using our sixth sense, ESP.

Now I will add a statement of information from Seth channeled by Jane Roberts as for all of Seth's information is so exuberant and through my own experiences has always proved to me as being right on.

Seth, "Your imagination of course fires your emotions, and it also follows your beliefs faithfully. As you think so you feel, and not the other way around." Knowing this is so important because when we realize that what we think is what creates our feelings then we can change our feelings by just changing our thoughts.

Now what does that have to do with telepathy, everything because THOUGHTS are what generate or trigger the FEELINGS, so it all comes from thoughts. As we can see as mentioned above that Fredric Myers changed "thought transference" to "telepathy" and so it is the same thing. Telepathy is picking thoughts from consciousness which is really being in the same frequency of similar thoughts.

Thought is like a tool we use as we sift through consciousness. Consciousness is everything and thought is what makes up consciousness so it is all part of the same thing. Just as an ice cube is still water just a different variation of properties in a different form, solid but made up of the same thing. Just as a pond or river or lake or ocean are different in size and variations they all still contain and are made of the same thing, water. So consciousness would be like the water and thoughts are different variations of the same thing. We use thoughts as a tool in consciousness to creating reality.

Telepathy Is Picking Thoughts from Consciousness

So then we realize that we choose the thoughts and we also choose the ones to pick up from too, different vibrations have different frequency ranges. Its dependent on what we pick up on like a receiver to what senders sends out, or vise versa.

Telepathy also occurs irrelevant of how distant the locations are apart from each other. Whether we are a block away, on the other side of the country or world, or in space or on the moon or anywhere in the Universe, it does not matter.

Whether we are the receiver receiving the messages or information or the sender sending the message, it is all in the mix of consciousness and thoughts. So we are really always sending and receiving all of the time. It's a tuning in and taking notice, as a channel that you pick up the information of the thoughts we are in similar frequency with.

We can also come to realize that telepathy is synchronicity of what is occurring as the external sign of our experience. When we think similar thoughts as another we become in the same frequency thought range and we will pick up on their thoughts or the information in that thought frequency. It's synchronicity which is being in the same vibration frequency that aligns the thoughts to show us the physical synch, same experience.

It's also referred to as entangled, as quantum physics experiments show and explain, consciousness of thoughts become entangled, in synch with one another. So it's dependent on what we tune into with our focus and awareness of our thoughts that will be the tuning in of the channeling of information we receive.

Chapter 3

✻ ✻ ✻ ✻ ✻ ✻ ✻ ✻ ✻ ✻ ✻ ✻

FIRE WALK

A fire walk experience really can change your limiting beliefs as it did for my brother and I. We were on a new journey in our lives and we wanted to discover more about ourselves and our desire to know about possibilities that were yet unknown for us to experience. We were excited as we drove to the city in Toronto to a seminar of teachers that were guided by Anthony Robbins.

The energy in the room was so uplifting and words are really a challenge to describe the feeling of it, so I will do what I explain on my web page about infinite words chapter. The energy in the room was incaptuallypassionlysatious, wow that felt good to feel and then create the descriptive word that expresses how it felt for me. The memory of the experience is still so fresh when I bring it back into my focus. Everyone was so pumped up and excited to experience whatever the seminar had in store for us. All my brother and I cared about was the fire walk, anything else was an added bonus.

The fire walk was the last discipline of the day, first we were guiding into a meditative state and I had my first aware full out of body experience.

The whole day consisted of disciplines and different exercises and one was to break an arrow with our throat and other disciplines and different exercises. The instructors guided and explained information about many expanding ideas and beliefs. Information letting us know that if one person can do something that may seem impossible, then another person can too.

Doing a Fire Walk Will Dissolve your Doubts about Many Beliefs You May have thought Impossible

When it was time for the fire walk we did another meditation or focus first, seeing our self successfully walking the hot burning coals. Then we stood in line and watched others go before us, one at a time one individual would walk the hot coals as we all cheered them on. Only a few individuals had a slight burn but everyone did it successfully.

It was my brother's turn and he stood there for a moment taking in deep breaths, I knew he was visualizing himself already successfully done the fire walk in his mind with those deep breaths, and then he went. As I watched him walk the whole way, he just glided through it. As I continued to observe the hot burning coals that were so red and hot I tried to not be intimidated by it and I knew if I continued to perceive it that way I would scare myself from doing it. So I stopped myself in those mid fearful thoughts and continued to tell myself, I can do this, I will do this, then visualized doing it in my mind again successfully.

It was my turn and I could feel my stomach starting to swirl around like that butterfly feeling inside. I continued to focus and imagine that I already successfully did the fire walk. Then my focus went back to hearing the crowd of students cheering me on. What a support group, I felt such love energy from them all. A bonding that grew from spending the day accomplishing such unknown experiences together.

That was it, it is now or never I thought to myself and I took in a couple deep breaths as I visualized one more time already successfully walking the fire walk of hot burning coals, seeing myself become one with them, loving them. At first I walked slowly. Then I felt some fear thoughts creeping in and I felt a tiny burn. I reminded myself within in second, no don't panic and quickly focused my thoughts back to focusing on as if I already did it, I did it, I did it, I continued to say in my mind. Taking my thoughts beyond into already accomplishing the fire walk, and then walked the remainder of the coals so easily.

What a rush feeling of accomplishment. As I felt my feet on the cool ground and jumped up and down with that clenching YES feeling with my hands. Wow! Talk about the natural feeling of being so high and uplifted! As the crowd of students cheered the next individual on, I checked my feet and found only one tiny little burn, which was probably from that one little doubt feeling when I first started to walk the hot burning coals. Just enough to prove to me that thoughts really do matter. It was not only for the fire walk but for everything else in my life in every way.

As my brother and I drove home we talked the whole way home about empowerment and everything we learned and experienced through the day.

That was over twenty years ago and it changed my life completely, it changed the way I perceived everything in the most empowering ways. Oh except for one other experience I had that was actually my first major experienced that took me on the journey that lead me to my divorce and then to the fire walk seminar which was the boating trip.

Chapter 4

✶ ✶ ✶ ✶ ✶ ✶ ✶ ✶ ✶ ✶ ✶ ✶

SPIRIT COMMUNICATION

I was a bit hesitant about going on a boating trip but my sons were so excited so I agreed. It was the start of a beautiful warm summer day. I awoke as the sun was just rising with its beautiful prism of color filling the sky. My husband at the time and my kids were all excited to spend a day trip on the waters of Lake Erie, with my sister and her husband and his brother. We all hurried around gathering all of our stuff we were taking with us.

We drove to the docking location and when I seen that the boat was allot smaller then I had expected, but convinced myself that it would be a fun day. We all gathered into it and headed off while my brother in law's brother steered us away from the shore.

The day was great, so warm and sunny all we could see was water all around us. Even the shore seemed like a distant dream that faded so far away. We came upon a very small island and docked upon it.

We had lunch and explored the island for a couple hours and then back on the boat we went again.

It was around four o'clock in the afternoon and all we could see was water all around us for what seemed like a long time, but the fun and relaxation was about to take a large transformation because the winds and the waves started to pick up. So we all decided it was time to head back to shore even though we could not even see any shore.

Fun turned to Panic and Almost Death

We were going along at a good speed of all of sudden the motor stopped and we were coasting along. My husband at the time and my brother in law and his brother all tried what seemed like such a long time tried to repair and get the motor going. But to no avail it just was not going to start. My two sons at the time were young, three and seven years young and of course the first thing I did was panic, seeing a nightmare unfolding. At the time I had no idea that thoughts created my reality but I had allot of spiritual beliefs and that is what kept me from freaking out too much.

First thing my brother in law's brother tried was the radio but that did not work either, the battery was dead too! OMG! The panic was really setting in now. No motor, no battery or radio, three flares, one paddle and only four life jackets. My sons both had life jackets on but we adults did not feel any need previous to this situation to put them on. The guys quickly gave my sister and I the left over two jackets to put on.

Now the winds were getting even stronger and the waves were not only rocking the boat but at also periodically coming into the boat. Now a storm had developed and we heard the loud thunder and lightening with some rain. The guys took turns doing the paddling with the one paddle we had, however it seemed as if we were going in circles. But they continued to take turns and kept paddling. They even let off the flares we had but there were no other boats around.

As all mothers instinctively try to be as calm as possible to not upset the kids in times of fright and that is what my sister and I were doing. Trying to hush my sons to sleep as it was becoming darker as night was coming upon us, we sang songs to calm our own nervousness too. Now we were in the dark trying to go somewhere yet without being able to see any land anywhere we were all getting disoriented and sea sick too.

We have been boating since early morning and now it was night time and I really could not find any hope to grab onto. My sons did fall asleep and the storm finally calmed down and we were floating endlessly in the dark.

Then a calm feeling took over me and it also was taken over with the others too. For myself I felt a surrendering as I never felt before in my life. I prayed and said to the Almighty Creator that if this is our time to pass on then so be it, I accept it and let go of all my fears. It just became to that ultimate desperation when there seems to be nothing else that can be done, that letting go and surrender then comes so naturally.

We continued to drift and believe it or not I don't recall any of us even having a watch to know what time it was. All we knew was it was dark and we were just floating. Periodically one of the guys would try to paddle again but they finally gave up the fight against the unpredictable waters of Lake Erie.

No wonder it has the name "Erie" in it, at the time I did not know that the lake is famous for its unpredictable nature and eerie it sure was.

So as I watched my sons sleep and everyone else was drained beyond desperation and settled in the calm surrendering state that seemed to take us all over, we all sat in silence. I think we were all silently praying and accepting our fate as we continued to drift and still with nothing but blackness and very little stars. It seemed like we were timeless not knowing how deep into the night we were without any watches to direct our way in the timelessness. It did feel like forever.

A Miracle Appears through Spirit Communication

All of a sudden as I looked far ahead of the boat I could see a bright light, I screamed so loud I woke my sons. I continued to ask the others and they could not see it, yet I could see it and it seemed to becoming brighter. Then I heard my grandmother's voice. This was my mother's mother, the other experience I had with telekinesis was with my dad's mother. I heard her voice as clear as if she was physically in front of me, she kept repeating in her Italian broken English accent, "Follow the light, follow the light and you will be alright." Not only did I hear her voice but I also seen her face so clearly, she also seemed so calm and happy too. I told the others that were still looking for the bright light and told them about what I just heard, seen and experienced of my grandmother.

My brother in law grabbed the paddle and started paddling as fast as he could and the others screamed that they were seeing it too. The guys took turns again paddling with all the energy they had left in them. It seemed like hours before we reached the spot where the bright light was shining. What was really freaky was that once we arrived at the location that we seen the light there was no light, it was as if it appeared and then disappeared once we came close to it.

We were all puzzled and looked at each other in silence. We just sat in the spot for awhile; the boat was barely moving as everything seemed to just be at calm, the water, the wind and the boat. It did not seem very long before we seen the sun rising in the horizon, it was becoming daylight and the dark night was finally over. Then to our right we seen a distant shore and the guys once again took turns paddling. I do not know how long it took us to finally reach the shore, we were so excited and wonder struck, time went so fast it seemed.

We reached the shore line but there was no docking for boats, we pulled the boat up onto the sandy shore and could see lines of house over a large hill in the horizon. The guys took to tracking up the hill while my sister and I and my sons stayed at the boat. My brother in law was the only one to come back as the other two took a taxi to get the vehicles that were at the original spot we had docked at. It was over a hundred kilometers from where we originally started out on the boat. We waited over an hour for them to come back with the vehicles.

News of my Grandmother's Passing

When we arrived home we were so ecstatic to be home safely even though we could still feel the motion of the waves of water for quite awhile until our equilibrium became back to normal. I called my parents, they were worried not hearing from us the night before and were so glad we were safe. My mom told me that my grandmother had passed away through the night and I just froze for a few minutes. Then continued to explain to my mom what happened and how it was her mom, my grandmother who somehow, someway shone a bright light for us to follow that brought us to safe land finally.

My mother continued to tell me what she heard on the news. That late this morning on Lake Erie a couple had died. It was because of the storm and they were found close to their boat in the water. Wow, my heart sunk and seemed to miss a few beats and my appreciation for life compounded a thousand fold from that news.

The Changes Followed

Life became so different in the way I perceived everything that I choose to live for myself and not be enslaved to anything I did not want to. I wanted to explore and do things that I have not done before, travel, be free and independent. As time went by I started to read empowering books and then my marriage fell apart as we grew apart day by day, as did many of my old friends too.

A new adventurous journey began and my life experiences since then has not stopped to evolve. No matter what the challenge is, it always becomes and opportunity to learn more about myself and evolving into more unknown. Going through that experience on the boat showed me that there is so much more to life that we can ever imagine, but it does take opening up to our IMAGINATION to know it.

CHAPTER 5

* * * * * * * * * * * * *

BREAKING ARROW WITH THROAT

Breaking an arrow with the softest part of my throat was done at the same Toronto seminar that we did the fire walk. The discipline was a couple hours before we did the fire walk and after we did karate chopping a thick board with our hand, which was another amazing experience for me.

First though I must tell you a short story about my son when he was young even before I attended the seminar, just out of the blue he was playing in the backyard and tried to chop a board with his hand. I ran out to the backyard because I heard him scream and crying for me. When I seen what he tried to do and his hand started swelling I took him to the hospital, back then I was not a self healer the result was that he sprained his hand.

Now back to the seminar

Before I did the chopping of the board at the seminar memories of my son's experience came back to me so clearly, just as the memory of a song comes back within a second of listening to a few notes. So again I quickly had to drop that memory thought and focus on the end result of the board being broken and then wala it did break in half.

It really was a most powerful one day seminar. I understand now the reasoning for all of the disciplines one after another as I have said before and you may already know that the brain rewires new connections whenever we do something that we have not done before. The more we do the unknown it becomes hardwired in our brain to be able to perform it again and again if we so desire to. In the seminar the more fears we break through and experience the easier each next thing does become.

For the arrow breaking discipline we were split into small groups and again went through visualizing the end result. I could hear the excited screams of others in the room as with our own group as everyone was accomplishing breaking their arrow. I was one of the last to do it. I tried it twice and as soon as I would feel the pricking of the arrow point against the soft part of my throat while I was pushing the other part against the wall and I would freeze up in fear. I just couldn't seem to get my thoughts past the fear and continued to see it puncturing my throat.

Getting Past the Fear is What it Took

The instructor came over to me and guided me on the importance of seeing it already broken, to let go of all fears and keep my focus on it done. The other participants were cheering me on and I finally just told myself I can do this, I will do this. Then I took a deep breath and visualized the arrow already broken like a video in my mind three or four times and then pressed with all my might. Then SNAP it went, broke right in half and my throat did not show any mark of the arrow pressure.

I was so amazed and that is the reason the fire walk seemed easier because the arrow breaking seemed more intense. The empowering feeling afterwards is truly amazing and so empowering.

Tolly Burkan not only teaches fire walking, he can also put a large darning needle through his hand and teaches others to do it too. I still have that to experience and it is on my list of disciplines. Tolly also teaches walking on broken glass and many more seeming impossible disciplines that are so empowering.

Chapter 6

✳ ✳ ✳ ✳ ✳ ✳ ✳ ✳ ✳ ✳ ✳ ✳

SPOON BENDING

Spoon bending or twisting can be a most powerful tool for showing ourselves what we believe about reality and the power we have in being the Creator of our Reality. It can show us just how much resistance we have in our beliefs, which are the thoughts we are thinking over and over again from our beliefs.

When we become to know that there is nothing we cannot do or have then it will always come back to our own self that is blocking or stopping the manifested reality into our experience.

Holding a metal spoon in our hands and feeling it become so soft, transforming it into a putty feeling from our intention, focus and belief.

It is easy enough to see when so many others have done it but it takes actually doing it yourself to feel the transformation for yourself. It can be very empowering and give us a different perspective of our own abilities.

Using spoon bending for your own feedback through awareness can show you how strong your resistance is in your beliefs. If you are able do the spoon bending the first time you hold the spoon in your hands that will show you how open and nonresistant you are to new abilities and possibilities.

If it takes hours of focus and practice that shows you are more stubborn and limited to what is possible. If it takes days or longer that shows a very limiting belief but the most important part is the knowing **it can be changed**, you can change those thoughts that will change those limited stubborn beliefs.

It's all about Change, Changing Our Thoughts to Possibilities …

I realized it really wasn't all about the end result except for when you are visualizing, already seeing the end result in your imagination and focus as the spoon bending already happened. Other then that, it's all about the process and what we can learn from it all

What do we believe is possible for not others but for ourselves?

Do not ever use any harsh judgments upon yourself for anything, including spoon bending because that is only going to detour your self further. Any tools that show our own feedback is a great path to our advancement, no matter how long it takes, the most important part is **never giving up!**

No matter what it is we desire to manifest, create in our reality, the most important part is holding that desire as already manifested in our mind and keeping the faith, knowing in trust that we will manifest it. When you know that you will not ever give up until you experience the manifestation ... then YOU WILL! The time it takes will always dependant on your own beliefs and we know that those beliefs can be changed.

Using Spoon Bending for Everything, Feeling the Transformation

The first time I twisted a spoon I felt the power, the transformation of the metal become so soft, really like hot putty in my fingers was amazing. This was no longer a metal spoon, this was a transformation of physical matter, molecules transforming into soft putty. Feeling and experiencing the transformation was the most powerful experience. It's wasn't about any physical force, it was all about the transformation that I was creating in the process. The metal became what I wanted it to become just from my focusing and intention.

The second time I went to twist another spoon it didn't happen until I focused again for awhile. So the first few days took practicing doing it over and over until I became to master it. What is really occurring is the brain is rewiring neurons of the new ability until it becomes hardwired in the brain. Once it does then we are able to do what took some time in no time. Just with the intention, it then is.

This works for everything!

Spoon twisting is a tool that we can use to show us how all creation works. Anything we ever could desire works the same way. Spoon bending show us just how it works in a physical feeling in our own hands as we transform it.

So no matter what it is you want in your life, whether it's healing your body in self healing, or more money, better relationships, better vehicle, better house, better life, it doesn't matter what it is, all that matters is your belief to receive it. Spoon bending can show you exactly what your beliefs are about everything.

It takes practicing as long as you have to until you finally experience what you want, you just don't give up until IT IS the way you want it to be.

One Last Important Part of the Spoon Bending Process can Show us all about Letting Go

Spoon bending shows us physically all about letting go! To be able to feel the actually feeling, sensation of the experience of letting go in our own hands, to feel the hard metal transforming and becoming soft is amazing. The experience allows us to experience the transformation and removes doubts about everything else we may have false beliefs about.

It can physically expand us to know how it works in everything we want when we are creating. For the desires we have not manifested in our lives yet it all will come down to not letting go. Just as in feeling it while spoon bending being the reason we have not manifested it yet that will be the final release to allow the manifestation to be received.

If you have focused, visualized the end result with enough intensity of emotional feelings and still have not manifested your big desires then it is the letting go that is needed to release so that your desire can manifested, be received.

Practicing spoon bending is the perfect tool to use for getting to know letting go in the most physical way because you really cannot bend or twist metal without letting go.

Chapter 7

✱ ✱ ✱ ✱ ✱ ✱ ✱ ✱ ✱ ✱ ✱ ✱

MASTERING CARDS

If you have already practice seeing through and mastering cards then you already know the great reflection of the practicing it can give us. The cards will show you so much about yourself. If you are not familiar with mastering cards, you will be amazed at the practice and feedback cards can show you.

Seeing Through Cards

The practice is using a deck of 52 playing cards face down so that the suits and numbers are not seen, then one by one you practice on predicting or creating the card to be what you seen in your mind. Once you get the knowing vision or feeling, you lift the card to see if it is a match.

It is not guessing!

This is very important because you do not want to cheat yourself out of the lessons and feedback that it will give you when you do it properly.

Henry Sugar the Book, the Story

In the book "The Wonderful Story of Henry Sugar" author Roald Dahl, one of the chapters is a wonderful story about a man named Henry Sugar who practices mastering to eventually seeing through a deck of 52 playing cards and how it changed his attitude and life. It is a fantastic heart felt story.

It is about the Feedback

It is about the practice and feedback mastering cards reflects back to you and your level of FOCUSING. Just as we do for any desire we want manifested, we quiet our mind and focus our intention, see it as we want it to be. We do the same thing with the cards, allow the card to show itself to you in your mind and then when you feel or get that knowing feeling, turn over the card.

If you were right on then it will show you how in the present moment you were and also your feedback for your trusting level of expectations too.

So do not rush through the deck, actually it is spending as much time as is right for you, regardless of the amount of time it takes before you turn over a card. It is a practice of focusing and creating.

If you are off by a number, as an example if you envisioned a 7 but it was a 8 or higher number then your thoughts are more focused in the future. If it was a 7 and you envisioned a 6 or lower, then your thoughts are more focused in the past. A 6 being only one number lower shows only a bit, maybe one vibration off from the present, one vibe into the past. More numbers off then you are spending more time and focusing on the past.

It is an exuberant feedback practice, mastering cards in showing how close you are at predicting the future, which in actuality is actually you creating the future. The prediction is only a linear perception of momentum of time in space, since we are really always creating. Predictions are an illusion and if we are focused in no time in the focus of the infinite dimension where all is simultaneously occurring.

So the time you spend doing the card discipline is a great practice for your own feedback of how long you can keep your focus on one thing. By continuing the practice you become better and better at seeing through the cards and also at focusing for longer periods of time.

As we know manifesting what we want in quicker time is something we all desire and it takes focusing with pure intention to do it and the reason that the card practice is a great tool.

An amazing website I came across, Vincent J. Daczynski writes about his amazing experiences with the most amazing individuals and Yogi's he has met that use supernatural abilities. In chapter one in his website you can read about the man with x-ray eyes man with x-ray eyes the man with x-ray eyes.

There are Ramtha students who have mastered the cards in one month to be able to see all 52 cards. It took the first student in mastering cards 3 years of practice to see through all 52 cards consistently. Now the record has been broken first by one student to do it in one month and now many students have done the same. It is important to also know that these students did not just practice for an hour or so a day, they practice for many hours a day, every day until they mastered all 52 cards consistently.

Greg Simmons on Beyond the Ordinary has mastered the cards in a month, also answers questions on Beyond the Ordinary about the cards and so much more. Though there is a small monthly fee for listening to the archives, it is so worth it.

The students would use another deck of cards until they could master the new deck and so on. Again, it's all about hardwiring the brain of the new practice mastered so it then can be done any time in the future.

Just as any other practice in physical reality, it takes time for the practice, then more practice for the brain's hardwiring so that it is a permanent memory to retrieve it. Unless you have become so masterful at shifting realities then it's only a thought away from mastering cards or anything else you desire.

In the beginning you may find it a bit frustrating, I know I did, but again this is all part of the reflection and self feedback to work from and responding differently to the eventual mastering cards. Also it will show yourself how committed you are to invest the time for yourself to expand in doing something at first is unknown to you.

You won't know how profound the practice of mastering the cards is until you experience it yourself and it may become a passion of yours to master it. Do let me know if you do master the cards, I am still practicing it myself.

Chapter 8

✳ ✳ ✳ ✳ ✳ ✳ ✳ ✳ ✳ ✳ ✳

TELEKINESIS

Telekinesis is the ability to become one, in others words become entangled as quantum physics shows with an external object and affect the properties of an object. Whether it is the movement of an object or the affect of an object to change it's functioning, it proves we are unified in the connection to everything. I have experienced it myself by focusing my attention for long periods of time and words to describe the experience is challenging because you really must have the experience for yourself to know how it feels to express how empowering and amazing it is.

Objects I Have Deliberately Affected

I am sharing some of my experiences of telekinesis as I never thought I would as I have not told many others about it, but since you are on this page then you are either a believer or curious enough to at least ponder the idea of telekinesis, affecting objects with your mind. You may already be doing it deliberately or desiring to do it. If you have not it's so worth the practicing because when you have the experience for yourself, all denial does dissolve completely. You just can't deny it when you experience telekinesis for yourself.

Keep in mind that the illusion conditions many to believe that we don't affect anything, however in reality beyond the illusions we are really affecting everything all of the time. Not aware that we are doing it until we become aware, just as we are creating all of our reality too. Awareness and experience makes all the difference in going beyond illusions into evolving into making the unknown known.

Everything we practice long enough with imagining focus, we are rewiring our brain which is creating new memories to then be triggered so that we can do what we have practiced and experienced any time we desire to.

The Water Pump
In the home I lived in before this one we had a water pump that became to not work properly. Most times when it should stop running after the water fills it is supposed to stop running. But it would continue to run and the only way to stop it was to manually turn the valve. Since I was researching and learning about how we affect our reality and objects too I started experimenting with objects and decided to use this challenge with the water pump as an experiment to see if I could affect it with my focused mind and energy. Instead of the normal way to just go and buy a new water pump.

Whenever the pump continued to run I will stop whatever I was doing and sit and focus for sometimes over a half hour, at first nothing and I would have to manually turn the valve to stop the pump from running. However after doing my imagining many times throughout the day and putting extreme focus on it and it did take weeks of doing this without giving up. I just knew I could do it and was not going to give up until I experienced myself affecting the water pump to stop running. Then one morning it worked, I focused as I have been doing for weeks, which was imagining in my mind the pump valve turning off and also in mind hearing the running water stop and it did, right on cue.

Well I was so excited and my hubby came running in the room wondering if I had won the lottery, as he had no idea what I have been practicing for weeks. When I told him he was very skeptical until a day later when I practice enough where I could do it on command, then he was amazed! Because I defied the odds of probability to be able to do it as many times on demand and it made him a believer. He is very open minded, he has to be to live with me.

I guess I became so good at it that I actually now affected the pump to not run when it was not supposed to. It went the totally opposite of what it originally was doing, now it would not run at all. So of course now I used this as another opportunity to practice, focus and imagine it to run when we needed water. This took more days of practice throughout the day until I was able to affect it to run by imagining it running and hearing and seeing it in my mind ... the water running.

Though I never got to the point of actually having a totally having a properly working pump because we moved from that home.

Computer Virus
A couple of years ago my computer got a virus, however I know that I affected it to begin with, energy is energy, and my fears became stronger then my no fear of getting one. However it was another opportunity i created to experiment again. At first I took it in to have it removed. But a day later it was still there! I know normally most would just take it back as it wasn't done properly, but I took it as a sign from my higher self to do this as I did the water pump.

I didn't put as much effort and time into it as I did with the water pump. But every single time I would go on my computer and see the message of a virus I would stop and imagine seeing the end result, the message saying virus removed completely and let go of all fear and filled my thoughts with absolute faith. This now became easy because I had the memory of the success with the water pump.

I would only focus for a few seconds and would let it go. Well it did take 3 months and one morning when I went on my computer, WALA! It was exactly as I had envisioned it to be, the screen popped up and said the virus is completed removed. Again I was so excited and my hubby runs into to see what all the excitement was about and again he was also amazed. It also amazed me how he is always around when these WALA's occur for his own evolving growth too.

My Car CD player

My CD player in my car is the original player since I bought the car second hand and it would play sometimes and other times it wouldn't no matter what I did. So I again used it as an opportunity to affect it deliberately to work, especially as I was going to be driving for over an hour or more and wanted to hear Abrahams CD on my travel.

I would envision the CD playing in my mind and actually hear Abraham's voice over and over. For the first 20 minutes nothing, the CD player would push out the CD and read ERROR. I was passionate, I was determined that I was going to affect the player to play. After 20 minutes of imaging with sound and site, WALA! It played! There are still times when it will not play and I put my intention into it, let go with the knowing it will and it does play when I do it. It is so against the odds of randomness because I experience it now on command.

You can read more experiments of people affecting random generators and more in the article "The Strange Properties of

Psychokinesis" originally published in Journal of Scientific Exploration.

When we deliberately intend to affect an object this is exactly what we are doing focusing our intent through our vibration to being one with the object through focusing our attention on it to affect it. When we know beyond the illusion that creates the belief that we are separate from everything we become to know that we are connected through consciousness and affecting everything we put our attention on long enough.

Telekinesis is one ability out of infinite abilities we all have the potential to do these remarkable abilities and many more. When we practice until we have our own experiences! It removes all denial and doubt when we have our own experiences of it, it's our own feedback as proof.

Chapter 9

✳ ✳ ✳ ✳ ✳ ✳ ✳ ✳ ✳ ✳ ✳ ✳ ✳

SHIFTING REALITIES

Whether you are aware of it or not, could we be shifting realities all the time? It can go unnoticed if we are thinking the same thoughts over and over because we will not notice much of it changing. Its changing even though it appears as if it is not or may have slight differences.

It's our perception that gives us the appearance of the illusion that it is a continuous line of events of reality, when under the illusion we are actually shifting realities, as if we were blinking in and out of them. Our perception can trick us to believe many things that are illusions.

Physical existence of our dimension is slowed down vibration frequencies and gives the illusion that our reality of experiences are occurring of past and future on a continuous range. And that we are in a continuous momentum of beginnings and endings. It is when we expand our perception beyond the normal perception and open up to expanding knowledge to know more about the nature of reality. Then we come to realize that everything is going on simultaneously, all at the same time. Past, present and future becomes not to be what in the past was understood to be true.

Thanks to quantum physics that has shown through many experiments that prove there is so much going on compared to what classic physics and science assumed. Now ancient knowledge that has been passed down by the greatest masters can have the scientific proof that it never had in the past.

How Our Present Awareness Can See Through Illusions

A great analogy that can show us how reality shifting is going on and how our present awareness can allow us to see through illusions is in watching an electrical fan. When a fan is switched off, the blades are clearly visible. If we switch it to a slow low speed we can still see the blades oscillating. But when we switch the fan to a high speed we can no longer see the blades oscillating, it appears as if the blades have disappeared. This analogy can be compared to lower vibration frequencies that give the illusion of past and future on a continuous perceived momentum compared to higher vibration frequencies of infinite realities and how we are shifting realities.

Our plane-t of existence is on a lower slower vibration frequency which we could also label as finite, like a fan switched on off or low speed of perception. Since we are always creating whether we are aware of the wisdom or not it is what we are doing, creating our manifestations through shifting realities.

Not perceiving beyond the lower frequencies will limit us from infinite perceptions of many labeled psychic powers because they will seem impossible in our beliefs. When we stop the chattering of our personalities as our altered ego we can become aware of the unlimited dimensions or realities.

The fan analogy compared to our perception allows us to see through the illusion to know the truth of what is really occurring. We do not assume that there are no blades or that they have disappeared just because we do not see them at high speed. This would be similar to assume that other realities are not there just because we cannot see them either and this is limiting our perceptions.

Keeping our self in present awareness at every opportunity can expand our self to perceive more then we are actually sensing our self to perceive. The more we see through the illusions of the lower frequencies of reality the more the illusions will fade. As the illusion fades it allow us to perceive shifting realities that were once in our past seeming invisible to us to be more visible. Then we can perceive the oscillating higher vibrations through our present awareness.

Shifting Realities to Your Preferences

How to shift realities to your preferences is done by thinking new thoughts compared to the old thoughts that you have been thinking. When you continue to do that until it becomes a habit then you will see your reality changing to what you prefer to be manifesting and become.

The tricky part is trying to beware and observing the slight alterations of the minute changes as your realities shift. It does take quite the focus and constant self observation to notice. I find it so amazing when I do notice and more and more proof from experience keeps unfolding in amazing ways.

Allowing your mind to open up with newer thoughts so that your beliefs can then come to support your expanding self and be aware of shifting realities. Once you start to expand you will notice synchronicities and little glimpses and glitches for yourself. Then you will start to notice that many desires you have had seem to unfold in your manifestations quicker and with more ease then ever before.

All it takes is keeping your thoughts focuses on what you want long enough and it does change everything. As you are shifting reality you become to love the reality that becomes manifested. Then continue to shift to even greater realities that you prefer and desire for your manifestations.

Shifting Realities Of Bliss On Your Way To Creating Your Manifested Desires

It is always a choice that you are making whether you are aware of it or not will make all the difference in the reality shifting you will find your life events in. It will appear as if your manifested reality will be unfolding in the creations you desired. If there is anything that you do not want in your reality then the knowledge of knowing that by thinking new thoughts will shift your reality to be what you do want. Denial of this wisdom will only perpetuate what you do not want to keep being created by shifting realities to ones you do not desire.

When we realize that all manifesting creations, which means all experiences we are experience is a manifestation from our own vibration frequency as Law of Attraction explains. Denial is just another illusion to create it to appear as if we can judge and blame others, which is never the case when we are present aware creators. That would be giving our power away.

If we want to change our reality to be as we desire to prefer it to be then reacting negatively would only continue to create the same experiences to be manifested. The only way to change our reality is to respond differently to it in our present awareness so that the reality will change. It will change its vibration frequency which is actually shifting realities to one of your preference. Depending oh how long you sustain the vibration will always be what the outcome of the manifestation and the reality that you will be experiencing.

Then you will be blissful through everything and your reality will continue shifting realities into more blissful vibration frequencies. You will perpetually be shifting realities to the creations and be in that blissful alignment. All day long and continue for as long as you sustain blissful thoughts.

It is always a winning experience because when we are no longer reacting in the same negative ways as we did in the past our reality is constantly shifting realities to our desires manifested. Instead of the continued shifting of what we do not desire to be manifested which will always be out of alignment with bliss

So as long as we are keeping our self in present awareness most of the time and responding in bliss to any experiences that we have created it will continue along the blissful shifting of realities. Then we will see our reality continue to change to what we do desire it to be and it will flow so easily.

I have been doing this for over two years daily and I now find that my reality continues to get better and better and more blissful. Every experience that was once a problem transformed into a challenge then into an opportunity to always keep myself in present awareness of how I am thinking and responding. And every experience changes is another learning tool that excels my growth into more expanding realities to experience. It surely is perpetual bliss.

All it takes is practicing it daily and then you realize that it is the new habitual way, so naturally that you will do it without having to remind yourself and simultaneously judgments are also becoming less and less. Bliss and peace become how you live every day so naturally and your desires manifest easily.

When we have Infinite Realities to Choose from in any Situation what do you Focus Upon?

Since we a choosing all of the time from infinite realities dependant on where we put our attention by focused thoughts and emotions that concentrates the energy of vibration to be tuned in or be in the frequency our the reality to become into physical.

We have available to us parallel infinite realities to choose from, so it is always to our benefit to choose the one we **prefer**, instead of the one we don't prefer to be our physical reality we will be experiencing. Remember that our linear perception of time and space gives us the illusion that everything is a linear momentum of past, present and future. This is the illusion that gives us no power when we believe that is the way true reality works. We take our power back when we see through the illusion by opening up our mind to the new teaching of reality and how flexible it really is.

In the video from the movie, "What the Bleep" illustrates how we have infinite possibilities until we collapse the wave function into a particle solidified state of reality we experience.

How my Wallet Experience gave me another Opportunity to put the Infinite Realities into Practice

An experience I would like to share with you of a situation that allowed me to sit back and observe to create the preferred reality I desired. The other day I went to our water filling station to fill jugs for clean drinking water. The filling station is the only one in our area and it's usually quite busy.

The other day I was the only one there and I had put my wallet on the pole near the jugs as I kept getting quarters out of my wallet. After I had filled all the jugs and put them in the truck I left and went home. I took the dog for a walk and just before relaxing realized my wallet was not in my purse.

It has been over an hour since I left the filling station and I assumed that many people must of come and gone from it within an hour. The 10 minute or more drive to the station was when the first fear thought surfaced that my wallet was probably gone and all my cash too. I love my wallet especially because it was a gift from my son and daughter-in-law.

It only took me a few seconds to remind myself that I have **infinite realities** to choose from and to choose the one I prefer to be the one I experience. I also reminded myself of the creation law, "what we put out we get back" so I knew that my energy in that context was good too. I know the odds would seem that the fear based reality would be the most logical one that created my wallet to be gone. I knew better and that I am a powerful being, which I reminded myself and choose to focus on what I preferred my reality to be.

So I pushed away the fear thoughts and focused like a video playing in my mind, calmly with absolute trust that my wallet was still sitting there as I left it, and no one else was there either. I did that over and over as I drove until I arrived at the road that the filling station was on. I also gave thanks in advance for my wallet being there.

As I drove closer to the entrance I seen a vehicle drive up to the traffic lights and knew they had to come out of the station, as there is no other road between the lights and the station. Yet I kept my focus and attention on what I preferred.

As I drove up to the pole, my wallet was there just where I left it. Then I checked through it and nothing had been touched it was just as I left it.

What if I would of Choose the Fear Reality?

We may wonder about the opposite choice of choosing the fear based reality of the wallet not being there. If I would of continued in focusing my thoughts with feelings in fear, anxiousness of my wallet not being there, would the reality have been different?

I think it would have been different, the wallet would not of been where I left it. Maybe more drama would have played out in my reality as it has in my past before knowing about shifting of realities. There are many possibilities that could of manifested as my reality, someone found the wallet and called me to return it. Or it could have been gone without a trace.

Always keeping in mind that it will dependant on our own belief systems of how our manifestations are created into physical. If parallel realities are true then it gives us the power to choose and no longer be a victim in our lives. Just from choosing what we prefer instead of what we do not prefer, two opposite vibrations that will create the reality we put the most energy into.

Whether we choose to believe in reality shifting or not, just the realization from our own proven experiences will show us that we have a choice and that does make all the difference.

"As within so without" in our Imagination First

Being Specific, Trusting and Giving Thanks in Advance Glues it all Together

I had experienced what I had envisioned with feeling, trust and thanks inwardly in my imagination first and it became an exact replica of my outer physical manifestation, exactly. I choose from the Source, Field, Vortex, Infinite Intelligence whatever you choose to label it as, it's a field of parallel infinite realities that is going on infinitely all the time.

Being very specific when we imagine whatever it is we desire to become manifested seems to really zoom our preference in with trusting in that knowing it will become, especially when we bless it with thanks and then becomes the created physical reality we experience.

For me it is not just this experience, it is doing it with everything throughout my day, leaving nothing out. It is when it becomes a practice we do all the time with everything and then it becomes so natural to live our lives this way. We leave nothing to chance because we become to know from our own experiences that chance is an illusion.

In creation there is only creating, no random chance, just creating by what we focus upon. And the biggest opportunities will always be using this practice of shifting through infinite realities and solidifying the one we want to experience in physical. It just takes some practicing long enough until it is hardwired in our brain.

Accepting what You do not Prefer

Accepting and giving thanks for the reality that you are living that you do not prefer or want keeps the higher vibration active. Realizing that any part of the reality you don't prefer is only left over residue from focused thoughts you gave attention to.

By giving thanks for the unwanted or not preferred reality, you are also vibrating energy of gratitude, appreciation that is a high vibration frequency. Appreciation that you realize now what you do want instead you will expand your high vibrations to add to what you are already putting out.

This is what Abraham says, "Making peace with where you are" and when we make peace with where we are we are allowing the door to open to bring more to appreciate. It also quickens our vibration to manifesting more of what we do want into our experiences. So whatever it is you don't prefer right now make peace with it and continue to insert the reality you do prefer.

It's by choosing from the parallel infinite realities that are already going on and solidify it by focusing with feelings upon it. Then it will become the physical reality you will be experiencing.

PART THREE

HELPFUL KNOWLEDGE TRANSFORMS DOUBTS

As we learn new knowledge and then experience what we have learned it transforms all doubt and becomes our own wisdom.

ANNAMARIE ANTOSKI

CHAPTER 1

✻ ✻ ✻ ✻ ✻ ✻ ✻ ✻ ✻ ✻ ✻ ✻

OUR BRAIN REWIRES ITSELF

Now that we have advanced in technology and are able to actually watch how our brain rewires itself when we practice and imagine ourselves doing something new.

We are doing the work inside, which seems invisible physically and our brain rewires through the process of our imagining. It hardwires the new pathways so that we can then experience it outwardly in physical reality.

Considering not too long ago it was believed that we were not able to grow new neurons. Until research, experiments and new technology was able to show us that indeed we do grow new pathways. By visualizing or imagining doing something new is the key to hardwiring the new memories.

What our Brain is Doing when we Practice and Imagine Something New

I am going to use spoon twisting as an example of doing something new. First we get the idea and then before we experience the physical reality of the idea we need to practice by imagining first. By quieting our mind and focusing on our new idea as already being what we would be experiencing in our physical reality. Which for spoon twisting it is seeing the spoon already twisted.

We must continue to imagine it until we do it, regardless of how long it takes. "Failure is not an option" in other words as long as we do not quit or give up we will succeed. Depending on our own unique beliefs will be the only factoring level of timing, level of acceptance amount before we actually experience it in physical.

The most important key here is practicing it long enough for the rewiring of the new pathways of neurons from the imagining it first and then the new beliefs will just naturally become to support the new experience. Then anytime you desire to perform the new experience, once it is hardwired, you can perform it anytime you desire. The memory is now hardwired for later recollecting.

In a video from Discovery they show we have over 100 billion neurons in our brain and connecting to 50,000 more, like an actual storm just as it's shown in the movie, "What the Bleep Do We Know" too.

Plasticity of the Brain

Here is a description from Wikipedia, "Neuroplasticity (also referred to as brain plasticity, cortical plasticity or cortical re-mapping) is the changing of neurons, the organization of their networks, and their function via new experiences. This idea was first proposed in 1890 by William James in The Principles of Psychology, though the idea was largely neglected for the next fifty years.[1] The first person to use the term neural plasticity appears to have been the Polish neuroscientist Jerzy Konorski."

"The brain consists of nerve cells (or "neurons") and glial cells which are interconnected, and learning may happen through change in the strength of the connections, by adding or removing connections, or by adding new cells. "Plasticity" relates to learning by adding or removing connections, or adding cells."

A great book by Norman Doidge, MD not only explains but also gives many examples of experiences of the brain that changes itself and years of research that has been done.

Anything becomes Possible when you Imagine it Long Enough

So then what is actually possible? That leaves actually nothing out!

Everything is possible when we expand our mind and expand our beliefs to accept that everything and anything is possible.

Let us delve into many of the paranormal experiences and practices that many masters have been telling us from what they are able to experience. Sai Baba is able to manifest anything in his hands within real time, instantly. Do we believe that is possible?

When you become into the knowing from your own experiences that have proven to yourself of any idea you have had that seemed impossible to you, until you were able to prove to yourself that it was possible. Once you experience the manifested reality for yourself then you know it is, no matter what it was that you desired.

These seemingly impossible manifestations are possible too, once we expand our consciousness to the reality and expand our beliefs, then we will become more comfortable with new ideas of what is possible.

This is the capability our brains do have to creating idea's that seem impossible to becoming possible for our own experience. All it takes is practicing long enough until we rewire the new pathways for us to experience it in physical.

Chapter 2

✳ ✳ ✳ ✳ ✳ ✳ ✳ ✳ ✳ ✳ ✳ ✳ ✳

CREATE YOUR DAY YOUR WAY

"I Create My Day" is popular from "What the Bleep" movie, it's a Ramtha teaching upon awakening to conscious awareness to giving our attention to how we want our day to be in it's unfolding manifesting of reality.

So at the beginning of your day you can actually write out a list of how you consciously choose to want your day to be created. Instead of leaving it up to chance, which is really leaving it up to automatic past programs of how we reacted in the past to be our present days creations.

By writing it down you are giving yourself more attention, awareness and focus on the list and then throughout the day you will also be noticing if it is being created the way you want it to be or not.

At anytime you can reinforce your day's creation by giving it conscious attention and focus with expectancy.

If you have never done this before then it will take some practice, but if you have done it then you already have a memory of it and it will become easier and easier until it becomes habitual. It's the most powerful way to start every day by knowing you are the one in control of how your day will be created

The Choice is Up to You!

You really do always have the choice to pick uplifting thoughts or downer thoughts and the powerful difference will be in what you choose either the negative or the positive. Or the love based thoughts that will trigger positive based feelings or fear based thoughts that will trigger negative feelings.

It is also a huge advantage to know as we create our day it can be from emotional addictions and that when we are aware we can insert better thoughts that create better feeling emotions. Knowing the choice is always up to our own free will, even when it seems it is not and that is where AWARENESS comes in. Choosing through awareness of what thoughts to give more attention and focus upon will literally also create your vibration frequency of what you will be attracting to you.

Reminding your self that there is no randomness or chance in creation, everything becomes to us by attraction of a similar frequency. So to not accept this is just plain old denial and means that you just are not ready yet to make that change or take that responsibility.

Since you are reading this then I know you have already desiring to step out of denial. Or just as I have you may too have already stepped out of denial and still have more work to do on mastering your day's creation bringing even more awareness into focus. You have come to use every negative as an opportunity to be the conscious creator and that's so empowering.

What Reality are You Interacting With?

Let's just try to comprehend for a few moments by expanding our consciousness a bit more of what quantum experiments have shown and many master teachers are teaching that we do switching realities all the time. That is even more powerful because that means that we are also switching with versions of ourselves and versions of others.

So for example for me yesterday was a downer day from not being aware and taking the time to turn my thoughts around it did have the domino affect. It also seemed that everyone I interacted with was also in some kind of downer mood too. Even though at the surface when I took notice that some individuals did have some good things to say there was still some complaining in the conversations?

Yet when I am in a great higher mood, others I interact with seem to be also in a higher or better mood and less complaining and more conversation about good things.

It seems that if we are not aware and only perceive in linear momentum then that is how it appears as if it is always the same version of everyone. Yet when we expand our minds more into the possibility of the reality of infinite realities and infinite versions and ponder in that for awhile, it does seem to make more sense.

Chapter 3

* * * * * * * * * * * *

EMOTIONAL ADDICTION

Many individuals are not aware of emotional addiction. We all know what addictions are and we know what emotions are too, but do you realize that we are addicted to our emotions? It will go unnoticed if we are not knowledgeable of what emotional addiction is and how it is running our behavior and life.

First let us take a closer look addiction and what starts the process to begin with. We become addicted to something by creating enough pleasure to it long enough that the brain then rewires it into something we believe we just have to have. Then it becomes habitual and an addiction.

Addiction really has gotten a bad rap because many addictions to alcohol, drugs and anything that changes our behavior in a negative way are attached with such negative beliefs. So the substance becomes the catalyst for our pleasure beyond anything else. Yet each individual's addictions will also have many different variations of beliefs depending on what the person believes about any substance.

The addiction that we are zeroing in on for this page is emotional addiction which really is so unnoticed because of the lack of knowledge about the interconnection of what we have attached to what we think and then feel. How it's rewired in our brain and throughout our body through peptides and through our nervous system.

A great book I read years ago even before seeing Candice Pert in the Bleep movie is her book "Molecules of Emotion"

When we release blame and judgment to knowledge and wisdom of how we actually create emotions and any addictions in our lives, we then break through all illusions to see how it became formed and how it works. This gives us empowerment because we then can work to create new higher emotions that will actually gives us infinite potential and radiate a higher vibration to everything in our life.

Many Kinds of Addiction

So we have substance addictions that everyone is aware of as drugs, alcohol and prescription drugs. Then we have addictions to food, money spending, love and so on, these addictions many are now aware of because of the publicity is has received, which in turn allows many individuals to be knowledgeable of it and work on it.

Now emotional addictions is coming to light as we are now finding out that many of our negative feelings were created the same way. So whether it is being addicted to anger, frustration or better emotional addictions to bliss, optimism and so on creates quite the difference in how our creations in our lives will be manifested. It also is what will energize other individuals of the same vibration to us as what we put out in vibration is what comes back to us.

We can deny it under the illusion that we have nothing to do with what pops into our life or realize that we are creating everything that pops into our life, negative or positive, it is still our own self that is doing the attracting of energy.

Nothing can have Power over You unless You Allow it to

This brings us finally to realizing that nothing can really have power over us unless we allow it to when we are aware of what is really going on. We make the choices when we become wise to what seemed in the past to just happen. We become to know that it always comes back to our own self to make those changes so that they are of the best potential for ourselves.

If we become angry and frustrated daily then through this knowledge we realize we do have a choice, though it may take some practice and work, we can change and override those old patterns of emotional addictions.

Each time we react in anger or frustration and become aware in our realization that it is an emotional addiction and change it by responding differently then in the past. This changes in the brain and the nervous system and the body cells and it changes the way our body responds to the new thoughts and feelings. Which in turn changes many illnesses and pain in our body as a result and it is what self healing is all about.

So the benefits of working on our emotional addiction being aware of our thoughts it's so amazing and will have powerful results not only in changing to creating the life we'd prefer but also creating a body that is healthy and in harmony with our better emotional feelings.

Chapter 4

✱ ✱ ✱ ✱ ✱ ✱ ✱ ✱ ✱ ✱ ✱ ✱

SUBCONSCIOUS MIND

I know, I know! We are all aware and have heard it all before that our subconscious mind stores our programs that create our beliefs. Yes we may be so aware of the information however are you taking notice of it on a daily basis?

If you are not, then you are letting 95% of the old programs that are your beliefs create your reality. If these subconscious programs are not in alignment with your desires then it will continue to keep you away from creating the reality you really do want. Self sabotage is one of the biggest results of out of alignment beliefs, that even if you create what you want, old programs create the sabotage effect in many ways.

We must remind ourselves that our subconscious programs or beliefs, our messages and ideas of what we believe as truths since we have been born. Using the famous analogy of an iceberg is the best visual to realize just how much of our hidden programs that we may not be aware of that is really running our life and creating our reality. The top of the iceberg can be similar to our conscious thoughts and below the water is similar to our subconscious thoughts of programs or beliefs.

Just stop for a few moments to really comprehend the intensity of 95% of the programs that may still be running your life without the awareness of it.

Subconscious Mind is like a Recorder?

Our subconscious mind is a recorder of data that has been recording programs since we were born. And the majority of the programs/beliefs are not even true, yet if we are still using them they will be out of alignment with what we desire to manifest in our life.

Imagine having a device that you have never erased but continually kept recording onto your whole life. Then any situation or experience can trigger the memory of the recorder in less then a second, just as you hear the first few seconds of a song, it will take you back 30 years in an instant. Time and space has no barriers at all!

It is the same as desiring lots of money and every time you get money, somehow some way it has to go back out, never allowing that extra to be around in your possession long. Or if someone says something that you perceive as hurtful, in an instant, irrelevant of time or space the subconscious memory of past hurts is triggered and brought to the surface for your instant reaction.

So if we are not paying close attention we will continue to bring up all of those old programs that in our present are so out of alignment with the reality we want to be creating.

Anger is another automatic reaction, so is doubt and hopelessness. Many self defeating programs that are stored in the old recordings are still sitting there for playback whenever we react in a negative or judgmental way. It has become so automatic, not conscious aware thinking which responding is, instead its just automatic programs that we are reacting from those old programs.

How to Change the Programs

1. Being Aware

We must bring them to the surface by being conscious (by being aware) of the old subconscious programs that are our beliefs. The only way to do that is to be as consciously aware of how we are **thinking, reacting** throughout our days.

2. Inserting the new programs.

By inserting the new programs we prefer to be the way we **respond** instead of the old reacting running programs/beliefs.

3. Doing the above 2 steps every day, all day.

This way you are constantly creating the change you desire consciously and will override the older subconscious programs and the newer ones will become habitual.

For the quickest easiest way to change that programming is to say f**k it!) as that really will get your subconscious attention to connect to conscious awareness because it interrupts it with some surprised or unexpected emotions. It can take creating a big enough breaking of the old programs. You will find if you have been working on this quite deliberately and consistently day to day that you have created new programs and your reactions have transformed into conscious aware responses instead, then you are on you way.

If you do not do this throughout every day then the programs will never be overridden and with the same programs running then the same reality is created continuously. To turn angry reactions into positive responses consciously we must interrupt the old patterns consistently until the new way to respond becomes automatic.

It also needs to be done throughout the day for everything or anything that has lower vibration energy of negativity until every negative reaction is transformed with an automatic positive response instead.

What this does to your reality is a complete turn around of opposites. Anger and judgment transforms into compassion then into empathy. Fears and doubts transforms into hope then belief then knowing of optimism and trust. The "I can't" transform into "I Can" and all old structure of illusionary reality starts to melt and transform into knowing you are creator or your reality and transforms into then becoming a loving deliberate creator.

What Happens to your Body?

Your body begins to heal, you feel better daily, no more aches and pains, illnesses vanish and your mood becomes more fun and light of bliss. Your body is actually responding from your transforming higher vibration thoughts, programs of beliefs. Your esteem and confidence becomes sustained and all faith is renewed.

The effects of your own self being aware and is a conscious way of responding has the most amazing effects for everything in your life. It flows through the totality of you! The subconscious starts to fill with the new thoughts, ideas that become the new powerful beliefs. The recordings of the old programs become almost desensitized as the new automatic habitual programs become the natural feel good way to respond to everything.

You feel how worth it is because your body is feeling great, your moods are great and you are feeling so naturally high most of the time. And you are noticing many more of what you want is becoming manifested.

Instead of being addicted to those old emotional disempowering triggers you have created new emotional triggers of compassion and empathy instead of anger, hurt, doubt or fears. Because your empathy sense is so turned on and habitual, all judgment becomes to have no emotional trigger for you because you now automatically respond with empathy.

How can one be in empathy and judge another? It just can't be done. When you are empathetic even the worse driver in the world that has cut you off you will have empathy for which removes the judgment.

The Benefits are Amazing!

Once you have worked on transforming your old reactions to new responses and have enough of the experiences that it has become so natural. When you're responding in the new loving ways and your body is feeling good all the time and so is your daily mood, you become to know it is so Worth It.

You become to realize that actually and absolutely nothing is even worth reacting the old ways because of how great you have felt more then the old running programs could ever do in comparison. It becomes your daily life now and it is easier then reacting from the old programs.

All it takes is doing it every day until it becomes the new programs and habit you enjoy more then anything else and it will feel exactly that way for you. It's worth the perceived challenges when you first start to do this because the challenges really do transform into a passionate fun way to transform your programs. Knowing that it transforms everything else a long the way.

Many of Bruce Lipton's book and video's he explains how our subconscious has been recording since birth.

Evolving into Paranormal Experiences

Any paranormal experience is making what is unknown in your beliefs to practicing them until you create new programs which are new memories in your brain. Using your imagination and focusing through enough practice until you actually have the experience in physical. If you have not experienced anything out of the norm then you have to create those subconscious memories to retrieve from to then create the experience for yourself. Once you do it expands your mind to empowering possibilities that you may have once believed were so impossible become possible.

Chapter 5

✸ ✸ ✸ ✸ ✸ ✸ ✸ ✸ ✸ ✸ ✸ ✸

EVERYTHING IS NEUTRAL

The teachings from the "Course In Miracles" teaches us to remove all meaning from everything. As our perception has been conditioned from beliefs that have been created from our separation from God or Infinite Creator.

Neutral meaning releases us from so many old programs, old beliefs, subconscious memories that have been valued and sustained throughout history and those old beliefs that are limiting and had so many fears, judgments and illusions to them. Just pondering the idea for awhile felt so uplifting as it removed barriers and blocks of what truth really is. It comes down to be is that truth is only as valid as the thoughts we choose to put value into it.

Neutral meaning is such a liberating concept that resonated to my heart and soul, making so much sense even as I still repeat it to my self anytime I need the reminder, that nothing has any meaning to it but the meaning we give it, everything really is neutral. And each one of us can give any different meaning to anything whenever we so choose to.

We have Infinite Freedom to Choose, Which Releases so Many Subconscious Programming almost Instantly

You know the subconscious old programs that store over 95% of the many limited beliefs of recordings. Well this wisdom of knowledge that everything is neutral wipes away or overrides so many of them in the quickest time.

So what is left to really believe in?

If everything is neutral and meaningless anyway does not mean we can just think and act negatively either, well we can but as we evolve into higher consciousness we come to realize that whatever we put out we will get back somewhere along our journey. So that wisdom in itself seems to take care of so much for us by keeping us 100% responsible for everything. The science of quantum physics has already proven that everything is energy including us, so it takes care of any recklessness in regards to pure love.

The Reason F**k it! Is coming up more and more often!

It became popular in the movie, "What the F**k (Bleep) do We Know" and now with John Parkin's seminar F**k it! Yes that's exactly what he teaches, F**k it, meaning to stop judging everything and let it all go to bring us into a neutral or peaceful state of being.

I know for years I used to say it and I am sure most of us have, however to create it into a seminar, what a fantastic idea that evolved so naturally for John Parkin.

It's all about breaking apart from the old paradigm, old suppose to be, say and do's and instead be our natural self. Just as swearing is defined to be negative with many attachments that others have given definitions and meaning with judgments. Swear words just as any other valued belief is a word that has attached meaning already to it and by creating a positive meaning to it, or keep it with no meaning whatsoever, we then change the perception.

To go beyond and be more creative we can create new words for new feelings we may have that do not have any definition because we are creating them and attaching our unique meanings.

It's all revolving from the same thing, that Nothing Matters and nothing has meaning built into it and beliefs are just thoughts we bought into at one time or another, "f**k it", all these statements are expanding us to evolve to our most natural higher self which is the neutral infinite creator we really are!

Creating us to see the light, so to speak, that we give meaning to everything and this gives us more power then ever in humanity's history. Knowing we are the empowered beings once we override all the old subconscious programs of beliefs. This becomes easier to do when we stop valuing all the old limiting beliefs or subconscious programs that no longer make sense to this new wisdom. We are the one's individually who are so creative and powerful, quoted from Abraham, "that we can choose bondage" if we want, which is so unconsciously subconscious that we even do that.

So f**k it all! Relieve all your stress which we know affects our body's natural harmony by saying f**k it when all hell is breaking loose. Or when we get to the points where we are putting too much focus and attention on the things we don't want that is creating what we don't want. It's the very reason to even say who cares because we are the powerful unconscious ones that have been putting all the meaning into everything anyway.

Chapter 6

✳ ✳ ✳ ✳ ✳ ✳ ✳ ✳ ✳ ✳ ✳ ✳

LEVEL OF ACCEPTANCE

It will still depend on your own level of acceptance as to the timing and then the ability to experience whatever you are practicing.

Example telekinesis which is the ability to move objects with your intention and energy may take a lot of practicing time because of the level of acceptance of the individual that is practicing. Yet another individual may be able to do it in no time at all because their acceptance level does not need any convincing for the conscious thought of belief system to accept it.

This is how practicing allows the time for the ability to become experienced in physical. The practicing is also expanding your level of acceptance by opening yourself up to more of the experience. It is really a comfort zone that continues to expand to become more comfortable through each stage of the psychic practicing.

Now that experiments have shown the plasticity of our brain and how our brain does rewire new connections when we practice and experience something new that we have not experienced in the past.

It is the exercise that every brain needs to keep itself fit and in great shape. Practicing any psychic or paranormal abilities can do just that for our brain. It is also very important even after you have experienced a psychic ability for example we can use spoon bending. Once you experience it once, you must keep doing it for a length of time until it hardwires in your brain connection. When you are able to bend or twist the spoon easily many times then it is hardwired in your brain whenever you choose to perform it at a later time you will be able to do it with the same ease.

When We Believe We Can We Keep Practicing When We Know We Can We Do It

My life took on some different paths and even though I continued to learn more about the nature of reality and I did incorporate it into my daily life to continue to learn and grow. It was the bigger adventures as mentioned above that can be a highlight in our lives as amazing feedback.

The first time I experienced my first spoon twisting it reminded me that that anything is possible when you believe, but when you KNOW you do it and it is a created reality. You expect it to be the manifested reality for you to experience because your level of acceptance has expanded. To feel the solid metal become like hot putty in my hands and then bend like it was nothing. Then to experience bending it with no physical force is just so fantastic and inspired my desire to expand to practice and use more of my psychic abilities.

Communicating with other loved ones that have passed on from this reality was another ability that became so easy and natural for me and the same with dream premonition, which is having a dream of a future event or experience of yourself or another. Most of us all have these experiences too, but many may just leave it up to the miracles of the mysterious.

Some skeptics may wonder and assume it is from our imagination, even though our imagination is in the realm vibration of infinite consciousness. Anything that is psychic or paranormal meaning out of the norm conscious beliefs of reality is from that higher vibration frequency consciousness.

Skeptics need to experience it for themselves so they can have their own proof because it is only by experiencing anything that we become to KNOW the validity of it.

To use an example it would be similar to visiting Elvis's home in Nashville. I have been there and for any of you reading this that have also been there know that the experience of the energy and feelings that come from that experience is so amazing that words cannot describe it. However, for me to explain it to someone else who has not been there would be different then actually experiencing it for there self. Just as showing you Nashville on a map is not the same experience as going to Nashville in person. This is similar to trying to explain psychic experience to a skeptic unless they experience it themselves. Or watch another perform something that seemed impossible become possible.

It is all there for us to tap into and use and it is all a part of our stages of evolving growth to become more unlimited in our beliefs and ideas of reality. By perpetually being open and expanding ourselves with infinite thoughts our level of acceptance expands into infinite creations and we will always find our self changing and expanding in amazing ways which creates an amazing reality.

Chapter 7

✳ ✳ ✳ ✳ ✳ ✳ ✳ ✳ ✳ ✳ ✳ ✳

LETTING GO

Letting go is such an important part of creating our reality into the desires we want manifested. It does become easier to understand when we observe and practice until we become to know the process from all of our experiences along the way.

Though it sounds simple it may not be as easy until we get quite proficient at letting go. Have you arrived at the same conclusion? The small desires that you could really care less about seem to manifest so quick and easily that you almost forgot that you desired it until you realize it manifested. Yet the big desires that you want seem to take so long in timing you wonder if it will ever become manifested.

The secret of letting go is in the paragraph above! Letting go does consist of truly what the words are defining to imply, to LET GO literally.

Have you ever desired to win the lottery? Aha I knew that would really get your attention and I am sure that most individuals do want to win the lottery, why not? That would be the most sovereign feedback of knowing we energized it and an exciting experience to be able to be financially free and spend money without any stress about it. And when we absolutely know that we do create all of our reality and nothing is ever left to chance then that does mean that everything and anything is possible even the lotteries.

Getting back to the letting go part of the creation process because again it is the most important part of the whole manifesting process. For me in the first few years when I started to learn about the nature of reality and that I did create every single bit of it, leaving nothing out.

It took me quite awhile to first allow myself to accept the idea as a belief. So it took allot of experimenting to actually see the proof for myself. And it took many years later to still understand the letting go part for the bigger things I wanted. But that is because of our beliefs that create the illusion, because if nothing is left out of creating our reality then nothing is excluded. Even though we may think we know, many times the seeming obvious things can go so unnoticed until we really keep our self aware.

Trusting is Knowing, all Doubt has Vanished

Letting go is knowing we are Infinite Creator's so we totally trust that our desire will be manifested. We become to trust from being aware from all other experiences of our previous manifestations. If any doubt comes in all we have to do it bring up memories of other manifestations we have created especially the manifestations that seemed so impossible at the time.

When we trust, we know that we have put the desire out. We have imagined with great specifics and with intense feelings. We continue to do it until anytime we the thought about our desire surfaces, we insert our feeling visualization again

Steps of Manifesting

1. The first part of manifesting is simple, you have a **DESIRE** and then start **thinking and feeling** by using your **imagin-ation** as if you are the **being** that already is the reality you desire.

Now here is the tricky part, without the ego part coming in to tell you its not possible, or you can't do it or this is silly nonsense or any putting yourself down and doubtful thoughts. Once we get past that part and the focusing of our desire becomes easy to put our attention on for five minutes, ten or fifteen minutes then its done. It is rewired in our brain as many master teachers explain. Then you just go along your day and act as if that is your reality.

Okay, yes you are right if you are thinking that is not so easy to do because your present reality is not that way yet.

2. Acting as if is an important step because if you do not **act as if** it is already the desire that you prefer, then you will keep getting the same old reality that you do not want. You are not letting go especially of the old reality you do not want. How then can the desired reality you want come through if you are not letting go of the old one long enough. In other words you are not being in the vibration of it being your reality of creation yet. It is a pretending game that you play with yourself. And it is what evolves into the BELIEF part of the process, because you must believe that it is possible before it can be possible for your desire to manifest.

If you have been manifesting quite proficiently now then you are already aware of these steps and will not even need this review. However I wanted to add this information in because it is such an essential part in creating the reality that is desired.

3. The most important part of the process can be the most challenging and the greatest opportunity to practice it until you really get to know how to let go. I know we all heard it a millions times, we even experienced it a million times yet do we really do it with the big desires?

It will always be what we really need the most that will be the most challenging until we change our perception and focusing about it, which means not needing it anymore. Yes it does seem like quite the paradox. Remember that sitting in a paradox can be very exuberant because it is like being in the eye of a tornado. No matter what is going on around it we would not be affected.

So **letting go** is the surrendering, the trusting that it is on its way. It is becoming closer for you to just be it to switch to it or whatever way you perceive it to be.

Trusting your self, the Infinite Intelligence, the realities are already there for the picking in the infinite dimensions to shift to by desiring it and believing it. Until you become the vibration of it and then next thing you will realize if you have done it correctly, it is the reality you become to be living. It is always from non physical to physical.

The letting go part I have found to be the most challenging for me especially in the first beginning years, you may have found that too. Even though all master teachers taught about letting go as the last step of manifesting or shifting realities that last part can seem tricky.

Looking back through hindsight I can easily see now how the process works but when I was confused about it, it was like trying to take candy off a little kid.

I would believe I was letting go of the big desires I wanted yet I can clearly see that I was doing the complete opposite. Wild horses could not drag me away from constantly hanging on so tight to it. Even when I really thought I was letting go, I was not.

I loved the analogy I heard years ago about when we plant a tree or seed if we keep going back to check it out to see if it is rooted firmly enough in the ground we are actually going to be upsetting the whole process.

I mean of course that made sense to me, yet I kept doing that same thing with the big desires I wanted. Yes pulling and tugging and yanking them apart and then I would sit there and wonder why I was not manifesting or shifting to my desired reality.

Planting my Own Trees

Planting seven trees showed me clearly how we can get in our own way. We dug the holes in the ground and then put the trees with its roots in place and then filled the dirt back in at each location. Then I watered the trees three times a week and after a few weeks just left them. Or I tried to!

Whenever we had fierce winds blowing, I would look out at the trees with such empathy and be concerned if they would withstand all that wind that would many times go on for days.

Where we live we are out in the open with hundreds of miles of fields all around. So when the winds pick up they really do become fierce. I realized that my own doubts I was projecting even if I was not going out and digging up the dirt, which would seem ridiculous to do, yet my old thought of doubting would take over and before I realized it I was putting out concern thoughts filled with doubts. And that is definitely not letting go and trusting.

As I sat and pondered I realized that if I did not go through all my adversities that challenged me throughout my life I would be too weak to survive and handle them all. It does make us stronger with each adversity we survive and excel from.

Since you probably also have been going through similar experiences too, as we are endowed with it as human nature to fear and doubt first. Until we turn it around so that the opposite becomes natural to us. But if you are not truly letting go then really knowing about the letting go step is crucial to creating your biggest desires to be created.

So I stopped my nonsense of not trusting nature and the trees and what they also had to go through so that their roots could become firmly rooted in the ground. They needed the fierce winds and all the storms to push them around just like we need our challenges to strengthen us. It is through that process that the trees gain their strength to firmly root themselves to the ground. I realized how my projected perception makes or breaks everything for manifesting.

So all of our own reflection we perceive outwardly of everyone and everything is filtered from our own beliefs. Everything we perceive is a reflection back to us of our own self and is the most exuberant learning tool I have learned from.

How I Created what I did not Want by Putting to much Focus in the Mix

All the trees we planted survived all the storms. But the largest tree in front of our house did not. When a fierce storm accompanied by a mini tornado whipped through just a fraction of our area it broke off half of our largest tree and did not affect any other newly planted trees.

I did not expect the strongest largest tree to be harmed because I believed it could handle the storms and the winds or did it? Until I thought back to when we just moved into our home and as I stared out at the big tree and wondered how it sustain these fierce winds. I seen a visual glimpse in my mind of its branches being destroyed. Then I reminded myself that if that is not what I want to be created then I must change my thoughts. That was a year previous to when the actual vision became reality in physical.

I wondered again, how? Just a bit of non realized thinking with emotion and then stopping it and letting it go and changing it could manifest the reality I did not want so easily.

There again is the secret. Without even realizing what I was doing and thinking I did let it go and did change the thoughts. When we planted the new trees just adding a bit more worry concern energy to the already mixture from the old worry thought really cooked it up.

It does not even matter the linear time gaps of our thoughts because when we remind our self that Infinite Dimensions, Infinite Intelligence, there is no time. Everything is going on simultaneously, which means that there is no tomorrow, no yesterdays, there is only present moment fluctuating momentum.

Something you give thoughts of focusing to five years ago and then give more focus to bit by bit, if you are not aware of it then it is adding to the mixture and is creating.

It may seem as a year or two or more has gone by but if we are not aware of how all the pieces do fit together into the mixture then everything appears to be under an illusion that everything just happens to us. If we are not connecting the dots throughout our physical linear perceptions of time to be observing of how it really does all fit together, we then will miss the most important parts for our feedback. When we do take notice and indeed realize how we did create the reality we did not want by adding more unaware fearful thoughts into the process.

This is what inspires me and sustains the inspiration to be so passionate in a perpetual learning from every reflection that I possibly can.

Let's Bake a Cake

I know from planting trees to now baking cakes, but hey everything has something to teach us when we are aware. I heard Abraham use the most exuberant analogy of ingredients of Tabasco sauce in a pie and our kitchen and it really does get to the crux of understanding how our thoughts really do matter and it is always up to us. And the flavor and humor that Abraham uses is just so inspiring and enjoying and keeps the fun in learning about our selves. Before I heard that teaching I had always compared it to a cake because I love cakes and many times repetition solidifies through its process to really rewire it into our brain so that we can be in the flow of our desired creations. So I am including my version of the cake analogy below.

If we compared it to an analogy of baking a cake, think of the mixing bowl as consciousness. It does have and does gather all thoughts without any range of judgments or ingredients as in the bowl. Anything can be put into the mixing bowl, but if you want a tasty cake then putting garlic and onion into the bowl will not give you what you desire as the outcome. Just as consciousness has all thoughts on a continuum, it is up to our own self to choose what range of thoughts as we would ingredients into our mixing bowl or created reality.

Let us assume that without realizing it you put in some garlic and garlic salt and it was mixed in the batter, it would be so difficult to try to take the garlic salt especially out. You could spend hours doing that and would still get a not a tasty cake when cooked. This is the same thing when we keep adding worry and doubtful thoughts into our mix of thoughts that we are choosing to focus upon. The longer you focus upon in would be how long your cooking time in the oven would be to cook the cake. The end result would be a cake that tasty of garlic, not what you wanted. If you over baked it by leaving it cooking in the heated oven over its appropriate cooking time it would burn and could burn to a crisp. Not tasty at all.

This can be perceived in the same way with our thoughts and not letting go when we should to get the desired reality we prefer.

Can you see the difference it will make if we were to just throw away the garlicky batter (fear based thoughts) from the mixing bowl (of consciousness) and washed the bowl (choose potential thoughts) clean. Then start over again in the present moment (clean mixing bowl) and continue with infinite potential thoughts (right cake ingredients) bake for the proper allotted time (focus on thoughts of the reality we want), then have the cake that is tasty (the end result). Not to take the cake out half way through its baking time and stir it all up again. I know that does sound ridiculous yet that is what we do when we are not letting go in the end process of the steps to manifesting our desired reality we want.

So by now you can see how tricky it can be in letting go when we hold on so tight that we can keep squashing it from circulation to allow our biggest most important desires we want. Like winning the big bucks of the lottery or having your body completely well and sustaining it. Or any desire that is of most importance that you do want. It will all matter in the last step of letting go of when and how it will become the manifested reality for you in physical. And anything that is not the way you want it to be is an OPPORTUNITY to do the process of baking your cake (focusing on the potential thoughts) until you experienced manifested as your preferred reality.

Now the famous statement "be careful of what you wish for" of what you are thinking about because Infinite Intelligence has no judgments. The most powerful thoughts with emotional feelings will be what wins out and becomes manifested or reality shifted to.

No judgments, so Infinite Intelligence only manifests it never judges, it is us that do the judging. Infinite Intelligence or the All That Is just gives and keeps giving infinitely. It is left to us to let go of our own judgments that can ruin the cake (our manifested desired reality from being experienced).

So the easiest and simplest way to let go is to not care anymore about the desire you want. Yes as much of a paradox is does seem like, it is the way letting go works. When we really do not care is when the blooming occurs.

How do we Know when it is Time to Let Go?

Is to not care anymore about the desire you want. Yes as much of a paradox is does seem like, it is the way letting go works. When we really do not care is when the blooming occurs.

The best way that I have found in knowing when it is time to surrender, to let go, is whenever the thought surfaces throughout the day of my desire, if there is any doubt, then I have not aced it, peaked it yet. Once this part is so natural and becomes so automatic and beyond believing to knowing and expecting it, then it is at its peak and just sit in receivership of your desire manifested.

.   If you can go a few days without any doubts at all surfacing whenever you think of your desire, then you are ready to let it go, you will get that knowing feeling. The most exuberant way to actually feel that surrendering feeling is in spoon twisting because you can actually feel the physical hard metal transforming only when you really know and let it go. To feel the surrendering and knowing in your physical hands is amazing and will show you surrendering, to let go in the physical sensation.

So to ride the letting go wave we must become the wave and enjoy the journey. Then when we least expect it, we are no longer hanging on to the wave, we notice we are the wave having the experience we desired.

Chapter 8

✱ ✱ ✱ ✱ ✱ ✱ ✱ ✱ ✱ ✱ ✱ ✱

BELIEFS ABOUT WEALTH

Wealth is not always about money even though when wealth is first mentioned it usually triggers attachments of money first. Wealth contains many more concepts then money and when we take a deeper look at our beliefs we can see what attachments we have associated with it.

By expanding our beliefs and perception about wealth we can allow it to be about so many things that usually is taken for granted. We can be wealthy in love, in great friendships, in our jobs, in our family and the services we offer to others or others offer to us. There is always a wealthy reservoir of knowledge to be found everywhere especially in the wealth of nature. Nature shows us how wealthy it is with all its abundance that perpetually multiplies.

This can be a very important catalyst concerning our beliefs about wealth because when we open to expand our beliefs and observing regarding wealth to include everything that is what we will receive in return. It does seem that its an absolute infinite law that the universe or infinite creator gives back what we put out in everything and usually over multiplies our return of getting back what we put out. So when we expand our beliefs to include all of this wealth of everything abundance is seen everywhere.

Wealth in Money

We all need money, it is our vehicle that we use for almost anything we want or need in life. Unless we are totally sovereign and have no need for money but for most of us that's not the case? Though if we desire to become sovereign beings eventually we realize it will take learning and experiencing more knowledge so that we can become sovereign beings. When we follow our infinite purposeful path we will eventually become sovereign in every way.

It is our beliefs that are creating our reality, whether we are aware of it or not and many of our beliefs can be out of synch with our desire for wealth.

Beliefs are flexible and can change as we experience new reality that was unknown to us until we experience that unknown to be known, then the trust is embedded to structure the new belief. If you are not wealthy then your beliefs about money are still in lack programming. That is easy enough to realize and is the first important step to creating wealth. Now all we need to do is change the program of beliefs so that the reality can change.

New Ideas about Wealth and Money

If someone gives you a gift you do not respond by saying no thanks I don't feel deserving of receiving it, do you? No, most of us feel grateful and receive the gift and open it. Yet when it comes to money or wealth we are doing the opposite, not being in the receivership energy because of the old beliefs that are still running the program.

We have to go back to being aware of what we are thinking and talking about daily as that will always show us what we are creating more of for our future which is being creating moment by moment. Do we complain often? Do we say ah poor so and so? That is more victim thinking from old beliefs.

It doesn't take long to do this kind of inventory, just a few hours in a day will show us what we put out. Whether its from our thoughts or conversations of words, its by taking notice our own belief system in action.

If it is in lack programs by being aware we then know what we believe. We realize that we must change the thoughts we are choosing and the words we are speaking to wealthy and prosperous thoughts and words. It will take practice and constant self observation every day. When we realize that our words are our end result of our beliefs and how essentially important it is to change old beliefs to new wealthy beliefs about money to keep the momentum going. Also reminding our self that we are deserving and that money, wealth and prosperity is our birth rite, not just for the chosen few.

As you use your imagination by visualizing, affirming, reminding yourself consistently throughout the day and how you react or respond in conversations about money? If its not wealthy energy then the moment you notice it, is the moment you change it too. You will become to realize after a few days and weeks that you have changed much of the old programming of beliefs to new empowering money and wealthy prosperous thoughts and words. Once that change has occurred then you have changed the old program and expect the reality to change. The new expectation does change the reality.

Does Visualization Work For Lottery Winning?

If you asked Cynthia Stafford she said that she visualized winning $112 million dollars from the California lottery, not just a few times but for over four months she made the choice and became obsessed with the thoughts of it and then let it go.

You can check out her interview from "the balancing act" that's on You Tube.

Cynthia is absolute proof that we can create the reality we want by keeping the faith. By believing into knowing and trusting in our desire. Visualizing, imagining your desire as already manifested and that knowing then creates the expectation that manifests the reality to become what you desired.

If we know and seen the proof in our own life that what we put our attention on does create reality, then we come to know that it doesn't only work for some things, it works for everything. We are always creating whether we are aware of it minutely or not.

The Illusion of Luck

Have you practiced using the lottery as your own feedback for your own belief system? It can be a great tool for feedback because it will show you your belief about luck, faith, deservingness and most importantly trusting your energy.

Luck is really an illusion because the nature of reality does not generate randomness as many experiments have proven. Nothing is random, everything is energy. What we believe and expect will be what we get, in other word what we will create. Remember it is seeing through illusions that gives us our power back to know we are the creator's creating our reality.

Wealth is also a part of that reality by either focusing our attention on lack or prosperity. This should inspire us to focus on what we do want and be aware of the thoughts we are choosing so it can create what we do want.

Notice the Abundance

What a trick our beliefs systems can play on us, tricking us to think that we do not have abundance. Though its amazing that we can have quite the proficient belief in lack. All we have to do is take a look around us and be grateful for it all. Just take a look at how many pairs of shoes, clothes, appliances, books, plates, cups and so on that's in and around your home. Then walk outside and take a look at the blades of grass, the trees, the birds, animals, clouds, stores and so on. We can see abundance everywhere when we focus to notice abundance, but we will not notice it if we are so locked into the lack belief. It's by noticing we will find more abundance.

Think of any vehicle you have purchased? Before you desired a certain vehicle you probably did not notice any others of its kind around until you became interested. Once you become interested your focus becomes open to see what has always been around.

The same thing is for money and wealth, it is all around us and we are the only one that is keeping it out of our focus. Once we start to put more attention and interest in wealth and prosperity we will notice more. And the more we notice the more we bring it closer to receive it too.

Money and Wealth Attitudes

Making potential money and wealth affirmations or words as a mantra will also help dissolve the old lack beliefs to bring it into knowing you can manifest anything you desire. If one person on the planet has won a lottery of wealth, then anyone has the same ability. The only thing getting in the way is an old running belief and the only person that can change it is your own self.

Any person who has won the lottery has thought, "I CAN & I will" enough about winning big even if they are not consciously aware of it themselves. They might say, "I can't believe it I won" yet subconsciously they just KNEW they would win. It is the only way that creating reality seems to work. There is no randomness, remember, so really there is no luck. Sure maybe the conscious mind of the ego personality believes in luck and randomness but when we know from our own experiences as proof that behind those illusion is creation. And the creator is YOU! Perceiving behind the illusion to knowing how the nature of reality works will always dissolve all the illusion beliefs that dictate the illusion.

People who are lucky believe they are lucky, luck has nothing to do with it because luck is the illusion. Behind the luck illusion is creating from beliefs of memories that have been valued and sustained. When we change the program the belief then changes too.

So what Program is still Running in Your Belief System?

Think of our beliefs as a magnet that is either pulling in to you or pushing away from you. The belief of lack is the magnet pushing away and the knowing is the pulling toward you. It will make all the difference in what you create for yourself of wealth of money or lack of it. Do you finally get something you want and then loose it the next day? This kind of experiences still has lack programming running that will always push things away. Beliefs like, "I knew it was too good to be true." These old beliefs of programs running will be creating the reality to manifest. Or "good things happen to those who wait" but how long can that waiting go on?

It takes a keen awareness on a daily basis to notice and keep changing any limiting belief that pops up. To use the analogy of weeds growing in our flower garden, if we just pull the weeds without getting the roots we will find that the old programs of beliefs will keep surfacing. To get to the root is to be aware as often as we can to get all of the weeds and transform them into blooming flowers, or money, or wealth trees.

Let's Plant Money Seeds of New Beliefs

Remember that old belief, "money doesn't grow on trees?" Well let's change that right now by noticing all the abundance of a tree. All the leaves, branches, roots below the ground, we can realize that the tree is already wealthy in abundance.

Find any tree that is in close proximity to you so that you can look at daily. Every time you look at the tree see the leaves as bills of money. Who says we can't have a money tree? When we know that anything is possible then what is stopping us. We are using our imagination to its most potential by creating triggers to associate with more wealth.

In just a few weeks of seeing all of the abundance of leaves on a tree and let that observation be associated to represent money, abundance, prosperity and wealth? AHA! You got it!

You will find that every tree you look upon will represent money and it will be a winning experience because every tree you will ever see will represent money and abundance. So if you pass fifty trees wherever you may travel you will be reminded fifty times and what does that do for your new programming beliefs? Amazing benefits! Fifty more times you would not have thought about money and wealth and those fifty more times creates more thoughts to energize. Do you see where this is all leading?

Bit by bit it will become natural! Bit by bit you will start to see money flowing and gravitating to you.

Chapter 9

✳ ✳ ✳ ✳ ✳ ✳ ✳ ✳ ✳ ✳ ✳ ✳

LOTTERY AS FEEDBACK

How often and how much money do you win from the lottery?

This simply will show you your own feedback of what your beliefs about money and your deservingness about money. When I started years ago, I used it as feedback and also intergraded all that I was learning into every part of my life and that included the lottery as feedback too. I realized that I had a belief that created unlucky tickets, no wins.

The feedback showed me that I did not believe I was lucky or deserving to win anything. When I became aware to notice my feedback and went to work to transform as many beliefs as I could about money and my deservingness and using the lottery was a great tool to show me about my beliefs. That was many years ago and it did take a lot of work on myself. I needed it because there were so many dysfunctional beliefs that were running my programs and creating my life. I realized that I could not receive unless I started to perceive myself differently.

It took writing out and reading affirmations every day to change my thoughts and my self talk and even the words that I used. I needed a total revamp and transformation of myself. Not only for my desire for more money, I also had to feel deserving to receive what I was asking for. Not only did I need self esteem but divine esteem which was what actually moved me to become to know that I am a creator and excited of the new wisdom.

By observing my beliefs about everything including the lottery. I found that the lottery feedback was teaching me a great deal about what I believed about money. First no wins at all, then I started to become luckier, winning lots and lots of free tickets and small wins. Then I started to win $100.00 wins and the feedback was showing me how my beliefs were changing. Now I felt lucky, not because of random luck, it was a result of choosing new winning, deserving thoughts. By choosing deserving thoughts it was changing my beliefs that changed my vibrations to be of a synchronistic vibration to create the matches.

If you are wondering if I won the big jackpots yet I have to admit I have not, but as I continue to create new beliefs that can support my desire is when it will manifest. However, as I wrote about on my wealth chapter, Cynthia Stafford won $112 million by visualizing and letting go.

When Winning is not Only about Money

I felt that I was winning in more ways then just about money. I was winning by my transforming my old unstuck for too long beliefs into new potential beliefs and that was very exciting for me and still is exciting and fun.

This is the benefit of being aware of old beliefs, it can show us what we do not want any longer and opens the door for us to know what we do want. So I became to love even my contrast and my challenges and many of my old sabotages and beliefs that were no longer serving me.

It was all a learning experience and feedback for my self. It also opened the door for new possibilities and knowledge that I can turn into wisdom from my own experiences. The lottery became a fun game of feedback and growth, just as we can use everything as feedback for ourselves.

Do you win more times then not winning?

You can change it!

By starting to see yourself as already winning, not just once or twice but through everything in every way every day. The lottery is no different then anything else in our lives that will show us feedback and transform ourselves by choosing potential thoughts. To become of a creator's esteem. To love yourself and know you are worth it, so that you can be in the receiving vibration frequency that will create everything you want.

There is no Randomness in Creating

The illusion of randomness, coincidence, it just happens or any other of those beliefs really are not true. When we know from having enough experiences that we do create our reality the illusions melt away.

Reality will appear in the illusion of appearing as random if we believe we are creating some things and then deny or doubt that we are not creating all the other experiences we don't desire. We will see through the illusion of randomness when we know we create all of our reality. If have the belief that we do not create all of our reality then we are still living in the illusion under a belief that is supporting that kind of thinking, old programs. But once we have enough proof for our own self from being aware and having so many experiences, there will be no doubt to deny it. Then we also come to the wisdom that nothing is random, everything is creation, being created.

Helene Hadsell has Won every Contest she Entered for over 50 Years

Helene Hadsell who is referred to as "The Winning Sage" has won every contest that she has ever entered. Just from reading Norman Vincent Peale's book was enough to convince her beliefs that she creates her reality. Helen explains in many of her sharing of her experiences that she visualizes, imagines herself already won and expect her wins. She says she sat in receivership and it manifested every time for her for over 50 years. She refers to as Wishcraft with her S.P.E.C. formula that represent Select-Project-Expect-Collect. She is so amazing and absolute proof that there is no randomness in winning, it's all energy.

Multiple Lottery Winners

We can also see the proof from lottery winners that have won not only 1 time, or 2 times but 3 or 4 and 5 times. That is not luck, randomness or it just happens, that is creating by the thoughts held in pure unaltered thought with no doubt. In other words it's creating the reality they desired so they had to have wealth thoughts energy to receive their wins.

There are so many more multiple winners that can be checked out on the internet that will give you enough proof that randomness has nothing to do with it once we see through the illusion.

We are creating reality by what we believe and what we believe depends on the thoughts we are choosing and thought about long enough. So to change any belief that is in opposition to winning, all we have to do is change the thoughts and think the new ones over and over until the belief then changes to ones we prefer.

Once we know how our brain rewires itself with the new memories then it's the same for anything new that we learn and practice. It is then part of our programming, part of memories.

Responding Differently then in the Past when Checking Lottery Tickets

Responding differently is something that Bashar teaches which made all the difference when I felt stuck in old beliefs or doubts. I was getting quite good at visualizing and feeling like a winner until it came time to check my tickets. When my normal wins of free tickets or small amounts would manifest but the big jackpot or big amounts were not manifesting I would so automatically become disappointed. It became quite a automatic habit and even though I knew I was creating the vibration that I didn't want, the automatic habit would take me over.

It took listening a few times to Bashar's video explaining the importance of responding differently then in the past until it was making sense to me. Then I intergraded that discipline into every area of my life too.

It really is so beneficial to use any new knowledge into everything in your life because just like the wisdom that we create all of our reality these other disciplines can be perceived as attachments to speed up the process.

How do you respond when you do not win on any lottery tickets? I am assuming since you are reading this you do play the lottery and hopefully not addictively either. I went through an addiction phase myself for a few months, years ago when I started playing the lottery. I was quick in realizing what was occurring and change it before it became another dysfunctional addiction. So if you also respond with disappointment then make it a playful fun opportunity to work on changing those responses with a fun, light attitude. Using it as exuberant feedback for yourself to keep the faith and trust in your desired creation.

I now am able to respond that way from practicing and noticing my feedback. If I allow myself to fall victim to the old ways, I quickly remind myself and respond with the best potential energy way. As Bashar explains that until we change how we respond from the past to respond differently to our reality, even if it stays the same. It's by responding differently that will be the momentum to the reality to eventually change to what we desire it to be.

When you buy and until the time you check your lottery tickets observe the way you think about money and the lottery?

I realize it's repeated over and over throughout this book and through all teachings that what we think and put our focus upon will be what is creating our reality to be manifested. Do you buy the tickets with the belief you can win? Or you will win? Or do you think about how big the odds are?

Be aware of the thoughts that pop up into your mind as they are the automatic thoughts. If they are in alignment with what you want, that's great, you're on the right vibration. If they are of lack, doubt and unworthiness then you can change them by being aware and choosing higher vibration thoughts until those thoughts become habitual.

This is a great article and You Tube video from Tolly Burkan about feedback when playing slot machines at the casino. He has actually created a casino slot machine seminar as you will see in this video from Inside Edition.

Everything can bee used for our own feedback, whether it's in Casino's or lottery games or anything else, its all feedback. It's all practicing through our own experiences to use as our own feedback to learn and know more about ourselves.

Using Lottery Scratch Tickets as Feedback of Your Vibration

I use lottery scratch tickets as my feedback to show me what vibration I am on. It is such great feedback for myself and shows me like a mirror reflection of my frequency I am vibrating. An example is if my lucky number is 10 and I need to scratch a 10 to get a match to win the prize amount but I scratch an 11 then I am one vibration, one channel off. If I am off by a couple numbers then I am off by a couple vibrations, a couple channels off.

We can compare channels of vibration frequency just as tuning in our television to specific channels to get the clear program we desire to watch. Scratch tickets can be the same type of thing for our own channeling of our own vibration frequency in how close or how far off we are in the vibration frequency of matching numbers.

It is all feedback when we perceive it that way. Then we can growth and expand from it all because we are being aware and also working to make the changes needed to be a vibration frequency match.

Just as you can use your drive in your vehicle as feedback too. How the interactions of other drivers and your experience along your travels can be used as feedback. All of your interactions with others around you, how you react or respond. Anything that becomes into your experience can be a game of feedback to show you everything about yourself.

By being aware you can make the changes necessary by changing how you respond from the awareness.

Chapter 10

✱ ✱ ✱ ✱ ✱ ✱ ✱ ✱ ✱ ✱ ✱ ✱

EVOLVING
TO
SOVEREIGNTY

Sovereignty in our past of humanity was only reserved for a small percentage of the elite. Leaving the rest of us believing to be enslaved and disempowered from our true divine, sovereign self. This has changed thanks to so many great leading edge sovereignty evolving leaders. They have been the catalyst that we resonated with because it is our divine heritage, encoded within us. Our planet has been enslaved to past history of genetics of the automatic programs that have been dictating our beliefs and lives of the thoughts and ideas that we must follow of what is good for us.

Listening in obedience to what we are told by the media, government and anyone else who is in some kind of authority above us. Under the illusion that everyone else knows more then we do left us not only with low self esteem but also triggering the same old memories of not feeling deserving triggered from fear.

The reason many of us are now leaving the old system behind, the old limiting beliefs and values that have disempowered humanity from knowledge and wisdom for too long. For the very reason that something just resonated with our hearts that we are much more then what they were telling us which is bringing our own personal sovereignty as aware creators back to empower our selves. The old ways have been losing its balance with fear tipping the scale and evolving in shifting to love to balance the vibration scale.

In the past it was leaked through from a very few individuals through time. It is now starting to explode because more and more sovereign beings are leading us into owning our own self by sharing their wisdom through their knowledge and experiences through their own evolution.

Evolutionary Leaders Gain Momentum as We Collectively Expand as We Shift into our Future World

Whether we attend the event or connect on line or just add our unified thoughts of what the event is all about. It's a way to expand into our collective consciousness and keep the momentum of the unified shift expanding. We are then creating the future reality we prefer by this focusing and by our intentions together, we all make a difference.

Individually as we interact in any way with our intentions to unify and collectively together energize our shifting world to creating it to be the most loving, unconditional accepting, allowing and empowering each of us to own our own self. This means to become to evolve to our own sovereignty. The more we know the more we grow and expand and the more we come to realize that we are all connected in the most energetic level under all illusion.

Time and Space without Linear Perception

So whether you are reading this page before the event or during the event or even years after the event, knowing that there is no linear time of past or future in the infinite mind of source allows you to still make a difference.

This means that even if you are reading this page 10 years from now that I am writing it, you are still expanding your focus of energy, your intentions into this event, even if it's of the past for you.

This is how amazing reality really is!

When we move our self into the infinite mind of everything, as remote viewing does, you are always creating a shift, a difference in reality. When it is deliberate through awareness of your intention and attention in the most unified and loving ways, you have helped and made a great shift. Not only for your own self in a sovereignty way but for all too as you collectively add to consciousness.

Infinite Abilities also Become in Our Awareness

We become to realize when we know that we really do affect physical matter by our thoughts and feelings we also can deliberately affect physical objects too.

This is also part of evolving personally when we realize how much latent abilities we still have the capacity and ability to use. While we evolve to creating life to become easier and easier with less efforts than the old

****

LOVING YOURSELF

Evolving Beyond the Belief of Conceit is to Love Yourself in Totality

I left this most important part of this book to last for a great reason. Since you have now come to the end of this book the journey will continue to unfold and I desired this part to be your beginning to consistently love yourself always. It is the most important journey through your perpetual evolution.

Louise Hay's Teaching of Loving Yourself

Louise Hay is the pioneer teacher of how to love yourself. In the video at the end of the loving yourself page on my website you can listen to her explain about how important and powerful loving yourself is.

Were you taught to love yourself? Most of us were not taught or role modeled how to love our self because of the resisting belief of conceit and so many other not worthy programs. Which is being a finite creators instead of an infinite creator. They, being anyone who taught or role modeled to you not to love yourself did not know the valuable wisdom of knowledge that loving ourselves is.

Since you are reading this then you are already on you path of loving yourself or you would not be expanding your self to the evolving journey of the infinite being that you know you are.

So we know that we must love our own self to be, have and do everything we desire. To be in the receivership of any of your desires you must love yourself enough to be in the vibration frequency of the receivership.

We have come to realize that conceit and any other resistant beliefs that's limiting is living/thinking from the ego or fear, resisting personality. When we have finally broken free from those old beliefs, then we have come to learn how to accept and love our self. Even if it's a step or day at a time, it's going in the loving direction.

The Mirror Exercise for Feedback, Louise Hay Teaching

The easiest way to know if you love yourself is to go up to a mirror and tell yourself how much you love and accept yourself. If you have never tried this exercise then you can try it right now. Simply go to a mirror and look into your own eyes and tell yourself genuinely from your heart how much you love yourself.

Were you able to do it without any resistance?

If you are years into your expanding journey in evolving in your life and loving yourself is something you have being doing for years, then there is no resistance. You already love yourself, you know you are a part of the All That Is, unified Source of Infinite Intelligence. If you felt too silly to do it, then the feedback is that your fear beliefs is running your life and the belief in conceit is still the program running.

It is a result of automatic beliefs through unawareness of the thoughts you are still choosing.

If you were able to go to the mirror and you told yourself you love yourself and felt some feeling of love in your heart, even if ego emotions surfaced you did move past some ego fears. Even if it felt uncomfortable the important expanding practice is that you did do it and when you continue to do it you will become more receptive the more you do it.

If tears came out then that is great too! Tears or crying is releasing of old build ups of old past not released yet, so tears flow then let it go as it will purify you in the process, it's such a releasing feeling.

It may take Practicing the Mirror Exercise for Awhile

Until you can look into the mirror comfortably and genuinely without any resistant of other thoughts surfacing, you may want to practice loving yourself daily. Until it is not only becomes comfortable but also genuine. By remembering that everything is inner first then outer, subjective then objective, "as within, so without", invisible then visible.

You must practice it until anytime you walk past a mirror you are able to love yourself regardless of any judgments, which means to love yourself with acceptance. If there is anything that you do not like about yourself, work on loving it so that the judgment is released. Then remind yourself that you can change anything you desire to.

Releasing of Judgments of Yourself then to Others

Anytime we judge our self it will lead us back into the lower vibration thoughts of the ego, of self hate or self doubt, dishonoring our self in some way. It's the old beliefs, old memories that will trigger any disempowering thoughts of our self. So it can sometimes be tricky, but by being self aware you are able to accept and love yourself bit by bit until it becomes a natural habit. By being aware whenever you start to judge yourself or put yourself down in anyway is the time to stop it in it's tracks and insert a non judgmental loving accepting thought about yourself.

Practicing the release of judgments on yourself is the eventual flow of releasing judgments also perceived in all others too. It is such an amazing experience! When you really work the practice to love yourself and eliminating self judgment into genuine acceptance, it is like a magical wand that transforms all you perceive and experience.

In all others, in situations and in all experiences, bit by bit you will notice the more you practice loving yourself and that releasing of judgments on yourself it will flow into everyone and everything eventually. This is where the Unity part evolves to come in to your world.

Loving Yourself is a Powerful Energy to be Vibrating

This great practice of loving yourself until you become to feel it within until it flows out, and it will. Using the analogy of a cup, when you fill a cup up with dirty water, you can see the cup is filled with dirty water. When you add clean water to the cup and continue to add the clean water, eventually the cup will transform to be filled with clean water, the dirty water becomes pushed out and the clean water then remains. This is the same way we clean ourselves up.

So the more we work on ourselves the more it will eventually reflect in everything we interact with and perceive in our reality and experiences. Everything starts to change by the newer vibration we are emitting into higher frequencies. This is what evolving from our ego altered personality to love yourself is connecting to your higher self into your infinite being is all about.

You will then find feedback in every area of your life. You will start to notice that you attract or encounter more loving individuals into your reality. You will notice less situations and experiences that would in the past frustrate and trigger anger will change and resolve. Literally your reality changes to reflect the new love energy that you are vibrating outward into frequencies of motion, your new reflection of love.

Loving that Loving Feeling ... Falling in Love with Yourself

We all love that loving feeling when we are first in love. Or when we manifest what we want. What does that loving feeling feel like? Lets immerse our memories into it. If you are not feeling that love feeling all day then this is a really important exercise to bring it back into your daily life.

What does that loving feeling feel like? It feels heavenly, blissful, like nothing can burst that bubble of lightness, carefree, on top of the world feeling. We see the beauty in everything, even things that were not so pleasing before just shines with beauty. It feels like we are walking on a cloud, smiley, happy, joyous, excited, passionate, free. Someone cuts you off in traffic and you smile at them and wave. It is a high vibration!

Nothing seems to be able to alter you from that blissful state, UNLESS you allow it by choosing some lower vibration thoughts to burst your bubble. You never have to let that happen. It is up to your own self to create it to be a habit from loving that love feeling enough.

Love yourself enough to be in that state of love no matter what is going on.

The more you are in that loving state, the more you will find less and less emotional addiction of the negative feelings. Those feelings that try to pull you into the alteration of your bliss, your loving reality of perceiving. It is all up to your own self.

What we See in Another, Is what we believe is missing in Our self

Whether it is something we seen in another that we want for our self, be it in a love relationship or any relationship or quality, negative or positive. We desire those qualities or whatever it is that you like or dislike about another, however the tricky part is that we believe we don't have it in our self that is the reason we want it or admire it or don't like it.

If it is something another has that you don't like, it is also something you may believe you don't have it in yourself, yet behind the illusion, you really do. So either way whether it is something you see in another you like or do not like, you would not be able to see either if you didn't already have it in your belief system, or your memory of programs.

The illusion is that it seems to be missing in you or that you are not like that, however we can never deny what we want or see in another being a reflection of what is inner first. The illusion of denial will make it appear as if it's not in us, however that is an illusion. The mere ability to perceive whatever it is we are perceiving about another or an experience or situation can only be perceived if it's already in us to begin with.

If it is something that you admire for example the success that another has, you have that same potential ability within you, you just have not believed you do, but you do. It just takes practicing to bring it out for you to realize it is there. The same is for an example of something you don't like about another, maybe the way they put others down, but if you notice that quality in another, then you also do have it somewhere in your memory too.

That does not mean once you realize that you have some of these judged not so good memories of beliers inside that you then judge and be hard on yourself. No instead you need to be more loving and compassionate to yourself, releasing the old pattern of judging yourself and instead love yourself. By doing this consistently you will notice more and more of your reality changing to your preferences.

Loving your Desires Into Manifestations

Do you fear, which is resisting your desires or do you really love your desires, which is allowing them to become manifested to you?

We all hear and know the difference in **resisting** compared to **allowing**, we can feel the differences when we are self aware. When we are resisting then we are worried, fearful, anxious, against the flow and so on … when we are accepting we are allowing, lovingly, in flow.

For any desire we want, no matter how big or small it is to our limited self, to the Infinite Creation it is all the same, nothing is impossible, everything is possible. It is only our beliefs that make it appear as something is a big manifestation compared to a smaller one. If we are in a resisting energy then we are creating our manifestations to be exactly of that energy, getting what we do not want.

If we are in a loving energy then we are creating our manifestations to be exactly of the energy of getting what we do want. Loving our desires is a high vibration frequency that also is a higher speed of manifesting it into our reality. We are not forcing, or tugging, instead we are loving it into being manifested. It is the difference in comparison to motivation compared to inspiration.

Have your Invisible Mirror with you at All Times is the Journey to Evolving

I found that by having my invisible mirror with me all the time, it reminds me of my passion of evolving into a love being. If I judge anyone or anything, my mirror reflection allows me to turn any negative into a positive or into love.

The greater the challenge the more you realize you need to do your inner work until you can then perceive it in the most loving way. Whether it is a person, thing or situation, anything is your mirror will show yourself your own reflection.

Loving Your Illnesses

If there is any pain or illness in your body, the first most important step is to love it instead of being in fear of it. Reminding our self that pain or illness in our body is a result of lack of self love which is fear. By loving what your body is communicating to you will shine the light on how to bring the harmony of self love to your body cells so they can heal.

Loving every part of your body unconditionally just because it's the creation of your beliefs whether its of pain or no pain, or the way you want your body to be or not be. You will find that you will have to eventually come back to loving yourself and your body first to bring the body cells back into its divine loving natural state.

Love your headache, love your eyes, appreciate your senses, love your heart and arms and feet and so on. Reminding yourself often that love and appreciation is the high vibration that our body's natural song is of love that will create it to be in tune or out of tune with love.

Becoming a Love Being

The journey to evolving into a love being does mean to love yourself first. It not only creates our life to become blissful along the way, heavenly on earth, it also allow us to be on the higher vibrational frequencies.

There is so much fun, excitement and passion on that high level and we also activate more of our higher abilities so that life becomes easier and easier, bewitching.

Yes, it become magical because when you become more sustained and fulfilled on that high vibration, more and more so called psychic abilities become interesting and possible in your new belief system. New creative ideas come forth and life then does become magical. There is tremendous benefits to being on the higher vibrations and when you do love yourself, it's the door way to getting you there.

Think of evolving as a baby learns to walk, we are learning to become love beings with super powers. It would appear to the norm as super powers but we know we had to take the journey to getting there. Super power takes genuine responsibility and it is so worth it.

✳ ✳ ✳ ✳ ✳ ✳ ✳ ✳ ✳ ✳ ✳ ✳

The Last Chapter Can Become Another Beginning

I hope you enjoyed your adventurous journey through the pages of my book as we shared our time together and remember to go to my website as I am adding pages often. If you have not been to my website before you can extend your journey while browsing and learning more intensively from all the video's and links on it.

If you have any questions or experiences that you would like to share with us, you can do so at the website.

As we continue to be open to more evolving consciousness of infinite possibilities to become known to us through experience we then become the wisdom. Also more possibilities will also open up for us to expand our selves into the leading edge to an even more magnificent amazing greater life of the Infinite Journey of Love.

…AnnaMarie …

ANNAMARIE ANTOSKI

✻ ✻ ✻ ✻ ✻ ✻ ✻ ✻ ✻ ✻ ✻ ✻

Pure In Eternity

Oh blessed one of infinity, I have finally arrived
As peaceful bliss not only surrounds me, is now beyond surreal
I feel it so whole and serene, just mellowing in all my senses
Caressed in the presence that is indescribably so real
In this moment of wholeness, connected with everything expanding
into eternity
Where the illusion of magic and miracles are only a breath
Though memories of the journey seemed like a rough and
struggling storm
Now I know it was worth every part to get me to here and now
Where I reside in eternity, moment by moment
Peace, love, heavenly bliss being one with it all…

I am the birds flying
I am the plane above
I am the river flowing
I am the rocks stuck in the mud
I am the wind that is fiercely blowing
I am the leaf that the winds is moving
I am the tree that is secure in the ground
I am each blade of grass that is turning green from brown
I am the dew that is wet and turning dry from the sun
I am the rainbow that was once so far
I am the others I see, hear and feel
I am all now that I have become whole in thee

INFINITE MANIFESTING

In this blissful now that is now extending forever
I am light and free exactly how it was suppose to be
Returning from once I came but now wrapped in wisdoms embodiment
I feel it, I know it, and the blessing is so expansive
I am one with it all, yet as I sit here quietly
I am moving yet so still in all that I am
I am that I am, I know and feel it
I celebrate with peaceful bliss for it to last forever

AnnaMarie

End Notes
References

Abraham-channeled by **Ester Hicks**
Website: http://www.abraham-hicks.com/

Sia Baba instant manifestations
Website: http://www.saibaba.org/

Bashar channeled by **Darryl Anka**
Website: http://bashar.org/

Giri Bala

Gregg Braden
Website: http://www.greggbraden.com/

Tolly Burkan
Website: http://www.tollyburkan.com/

Tom Campbell My Big Toe Books
Website: http://www.my-big-toe.com/

Dale Carnegie
Website: http://www.dalecarnegie.com/

Course In Miracles Book
Dr. Helen Schucman
Website: http://acim.org/

Vincent Daczynski featured in the What If The Movie
Website: http://www.amazingabilities.com/

Wayne Dyer
Website: http://www.drwaynedyer.com/

Burt Goldman Quantum Jumping
Website: http://www.burtgoldman.com/

Louise Hay
Website: http://www.louisehay.com/

Dr. Ihaleakala **Hew Len**
Website: http://www.hooponopono.org/

Bruce Lipton
Website: http://www.brucelipton.com/

Monroe Institute
Website: http://www.monroeinstitute.org/

Plaiades channeled by **Barbara Marciniak**
Website: http://www.pleiadians.com/

John Parkin F**k It Seminars
http://www.thefuckitway.com/

Ramtha Channeled by **J. Z. Knight**
Website: http://www.ramtha.com/

Seth channeled by **Jane Roberts** transcribed by Robert Butt
Website: http://www.sethcenter.com/

James Sinclair What If The Movie
Website: http://www.whatifthemovie.tv/

Joe Vitale
Website: http://www.mrfire.com/

Nicole Whitney News for the Soul talk radio
Website: http://www.newsforthesoul.com/

Wikipedia
Website: http://www.wikipedia.org/

White Christmas, the movie
Song, Count Your Blessings,
Bing Crosby and **Rosemary Clooney**

Also by AnnaMarie Antoski

The Hidden Key Orgasm Reveals
The Evolving Reality of Bewitched
Stumbling Through Infinity ... Heart Reflection Poetry

ABOUT THE AUTHOR

AnnaMarie Antoski has studied the nature of reality for over 20 years with consistent passion and has integrated what she has learned into her life experiences. Sharing her self healing and psychic abilities she has become an inspiration in her field of experiences.

Website ... http://www.infinite-manifesting.org/